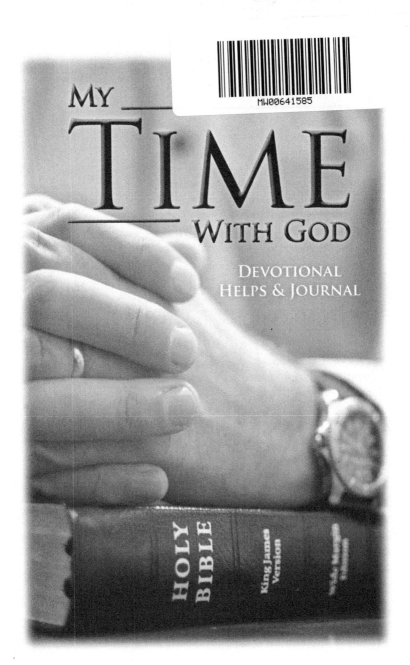

MY

TIME
WITH GOD

DEVOTIONAL
HELPS & JOURNAL

HOLY
BIBLE

King James
Version

PUBLISHED BY

HELP4U PUBLICATIONS
CHESTERTON, IN

HELP4U
PUBLICATIONS

My Time with God: Devotional Helps & Journal
by David J. Olson
Copyright©2012 by David J. Olson

ISBN 978-1-940089-01-0

www.help4Upublications.com

Credits: Photos from Ray Reuben Photography
          Cover Design by Joshua Barzon

All Scripture quotations are from the *King James Bible.*

Contents

Introduction

Life is complicated, and to make the journey through this wicked world we need a guide. Getting saved not only secures a home in heaven but also helps in this life, too. The Lord has promised to lead us day by day. His Word, the Bible, provides illumination for each step of the way. The Psalmist testified, *"Thy word is a lamp unto my feet, and a light unto my path"* (Psalm 119:105). Although darkness is all around, we can see clearly by seeking guidance from the Bible.

Receiving Jesus Christ makes us children of God. As a Father, God promises to instruct us, provide for us, and correct us. Each child of God is responsible to listen to the Heavenly Father. As we study the Scriptures, we gain insight on how to obey and please Him. When our life is pleasing to Him our prayers become more effective.

Developing a proper relationship with our Father is extremely important. Like any relationship, there must be communication. God must speak to us, and we must speak to Him. He speaks to us through the Bible, and we speak to Him through prayer. Therefore, we will fail to be good children if we fail to have a daily time with the Lord.

As you read God's Word, you will begin to gain wisdom and strength to face life's challenges. You will learn about your sinfulness and how to have victory over it.

It is my hope that this book will help you become consistent with spending time with God on a daily basis.

Dave Olson

"As newborn babes, desire the sincere milk of the word, that ye may grow thereby" (I Peter 2:2).

Tips for Using this Book

This book provides tools to enable you to become consistent in your personal devotions. Follow these tips:

Develop a Prayer List

Your *Daily Prayer List* has several headings with spaces for you to fill in your requests. For instance, under the *Family* heading you can list members of your family or particular needs of the family. Under the *Personal* heading, you should write down the areas of your life in which you need help from God. When God speaks to you from His Word, it is wise to write it down and continue to pray about it. This will keep you focused on getting assistance from the Lord with your problems. Your *Weekly Prayer List* has blank headings for you to complete as you see fit. It is impossible to pray for everything every day. Therefore, having a weekly list allows you to spend a little extra time once or twice a week to cover requests that you can't pray for every day. As you develop your prayer life, your prayer list will change. The prayer lists provided in this book are simply a guide to get you started. Expand and make changes as the Lord leads you! Lists help you remember what to pray for, but they can lead to mindless reciting of requests with no heartfelt urgency. So, beware of letting your prayers become stale!

Choose a Reading Schedule

Choose how to use the *Daily Bible Reading Schedule*. If you are just starting out, it is always best to begin in the New Testament. By following the listed readings, you can complete the entire New Testament in one year! That will bring a great sense of accomplishment. By reading the Old Testament selections, in addition to the New Testament, you will complete the entire Bible in one year. This is a lot to read in one day; but if you do some of the Old Testament reading in the evening, it is easier.

Study Topics You Need

Use the *Where to Look in the Bible* section when you need to study certain subjects. This is also a great place to find verses to memorize. Simply find a subject you need help with, look up several verses, and choose one or more verses to start memorizing. You will be surprised to see how God will remind you of His Word when you need help throughout the day! Don't forget to review your memory verses from time to time. This section can also be used for personal study or family devotions.

Keep a Journal

Use the *Journal Page* section to help you keep track of how God speaks to your heart. When you want to find a special passage of Scripture that spoke to your heart, just go back to your notes and you will find the reference for the Bible verse. Also, at the top of each *Journal Page*, there are a few lines for special prayer requests for that particular week. If you have an important meeting or event, you can list it there to ensure you will pray for it throughout the week.

Record God's Blessings

Record God's blessings to you in the *Blessings and Answers to Prayer* section. Simply record the date and the event of God's blessing upon your life. It is always good to review this section from time to time to remember how good God has been to you. When you get discouraged, these blessings will lift your spirits and remind you that God can bless you once again as He has in the past. Having such a record as this enables you to *Count Your Blessings*!

Learn Word Meanings

Look up the meanings of words you do not understand. A small dictionary of uncommon words in the King James Bible is included in this book. A Bible dictionary or old English dictionary can be of great assistance, too.

Become Accountable

Find someone to keep you accountable. The best way to keep having daily devotions is to report to someone each week. Let them check your book to see if you have completed your *Journal Page*. Additionally, you can quote any verses you have been memorizing during the week. Knowing you have to recite them will force you to study better! You can ask your pastor, assistant pastor, youth pastor, Sunday School teacher, spouse, parent, or friend to help you.

Help your Children with Their Devotions

Use this book to help your children with their devotions. Parents can use the *Journal Page* section of the book to assign passages of Scripture for each child to read and verses to memorize. Then, check their progress weekly.

Instructions for Spending Time with God

1. Start with a short prayer.

   ✓ Thank the Lord for His many blessings.
   ✓ Ask for forgiveness of any known sins. (Examples: selfishness, laziness, anger, fear, lying, bad thoughts, pride, lust, *etc.*)
   ✓ Ask Him to teach you something from the Bible.

2. Read your Bible and think about it.

   ✓ Look for a message from God to you every day. (Example: a promise, a warning, a blessing, a command, or a fact about God)
   ✓ The *Daily Bible Reading Schedule* starts on page 12.

3. Write down God's message to you for each day to help you remember! (*Journal Page* starts on page 44.)

4. Choose a memory verse for the week and say it five times every morning. (You can find verses to memorize from the *Where to Look in the Bible* section starting on page 24.)

5. Have some time for prayer.

   ✓ Pray for things on your daily prayer list.
   ✓ Pray for things on your special weekly list.
   ✓ Ask Jesus to help you each day! EXPECT HIS HELP!

6. Record any blessings or answers to prayer on the pages in the back of this book (starting on page 148).

Daily Prayer List

FAMILY

PERSONAL

FRIENDS

SALVATION

Daily Prayer List

HEALTH

CHURCH LEADERS

CHURCH MINISTRIES

MISSIONARIES

GOVERNMENT LEADERS

Weekly Prayer List

SUBJECT:

SUBJECT:

SUBJECT:

SUBJECT:

SUBJECT:

Daily Bible Reading Schedule

JANUARY			
Day	New Testament	Old Testament (a.m.)	Old Testament (p.m.)
1	Matthew 1	Genesis 1-2	Job 1:1-12
2	Matthew 2	Genesis 3-4	Job 1:13-22
3	Matthew 3	Genesis 5-6	Job 2
4	Matthew 4	Genesis 7-8	Job 3
5	Matthew 5:1-20	Genesis 9-10	Job 4
6	Matthew 5:21-48	Genesis 11-12	Job 5
7	Matthew 6	Genesis 13-15	Job 6
8	Matthew 7	Genesis 16-17	Job 7
9	Matthew 8	Genesis 18-19	Job 8
10	Matthew 9:1-17	Genesis 20-21	Job 9
11	Matthew 9:18-38	Genesis 22-23	Job 10
12	Matthew 10:1-20	Genesis 24	Job 11
13	Matthew 10:21-42	Genesis 25-26	Job 12
14	Matthew 11	Genesis 27	Job 13
15	Matthew 12:1-21	Genesis 28-29	Job 14
16	Matthew 12:22-50	Genesis 30	Job 15
17	Matthew 13:1-30	Genesis 31	Job 16
18	Matthew 13:31-58	Genesis 32-33	Job 17
19	Matthew 14	Genesis 34-35	Job 18
20	Matthew 15:1-20	Genesis 36	Job 19
21	Matthew 15:21-39	Genesis 37-38	Job 20
22	Matthew 16	Genesis 39-40	Job 21
23	Matthew 17	Genesis 41	Job 22
24	Matthew 18:1-19	Genesis 42-43	Job 23
25	Matthew 18:20-35	Genesis 44-45	Job 24
26	Matthew 19	Genesis 46-47	Job 25
27	Matthew 20:1-16	Genesis 48-49	Job 26
28	Matthew 20:17-34	Genesis 50	Job 27
29	Matthew 21:1-22	Exodus 1-2	Job 28
30	Matthew 21:23-46	Exodus 3	Job 29
31	Matthew 22:1-22	Exodus 4-5	Job 30

Daily Bible Reading Schedule

Day	New Testament	Old Testament (a.m.)	Old Testament (p.m.)
FEBRUARY			
1	Matthew 22:23-46	Exodus 6-7	Job 31
2	Matthew 23:1-22	Exodus 8-9	Job 32
3	Matthew 23:23-39	Exodus 10-11	Job 33
4	Matthew 24:1-25	Exodus 12	Job 34
5	Matthew 24:26-51	Exodus 13-14	Job 35
6	Matthew 25:1-30	Exodus 15-16	Job 36
7	Matthew 25:31-46	Exodus 17-18	Job 37
8	Matthew 26:1-30	Exodus 19-20	Job 38
9	Matthew 26:31-56	Exodus 21-22	Job 39
10	Matthew 26:57-75	Exodus 23-24	Job 40
11	Matthew 27:1-25	Exodus 25-26	Job 41
12	Matthew 27:26-44	Exodus 27-28	Job 42
13	Matthew 27:45-66	Exodus 29	Psalm 1
14	Matthew 28	Exodus 30-31	Psalm 2
15	Mark 1:1-20	Exodus 32-33	Psalm 3
16	Mark 1:21-45	Exodus 34-35	Psalm 4
17	Mark 2	Exodus 36	Psalm 5
18	Mark 3	Exodus 37-38	Psalm 6
19	Mark 4:1-20	Exodus 39	Psalm 7
20	Mark 4:21-41	Exodus 40	Psalm 8
21	Mark 5:1-20	Leviticus 1-2	Psalm 9
22	Mark 5:21-43	Leviticus 3-4	Psalm 10
23	Mark 6:1-29	Leviticus 5-6	Psalm 11
24	Mark 6:30-56	Leviticus 7	Psalm 12
25	Mark 7:1-19	Leviticus 8	Psalm 13
26	Mark 7:20-37	Leviticus 9-10	Psalm 14
27	Mark 8:1-21	Leviticus 11-12	Psalm 15
28	Mark 8:22-38	Leviticus 13	Psalm 16
29	Read Favorite Chapters		

Daily Bible Reading Schedule

MARCH			
Day	New Testament	Old Testament (a.m.)	Old Testament (p.m.)
1	Mark 9:1-29	Leviticus 14	Psalm 17
2	Mark 9:30-50	Leviticus 15-16	Psalm 18:1-26
3	Mark 10:1-27	Leviticus 17-18	Psalm 18:27-50
4	Mark 10:28-52	Leviticus 19-20	Psalm 19
5	Mark 11	Leviticus 21-22	Psalm 20
6	Mark 12:1-27	Leviticus 23-24	Psalm 21
7	Mark 12:28-44	Leviticus 25	Psalm 22:1-21
8	Mark 13	Leviticus 26	Psalm 22:22-31
9	Mark 14:1-26	Leviticus 27	Psalm 23
10	Mark 14:27-50	Numbers 1	Psalm 24
11	Mark 14:51-72	Numbers 2	Psalm 25
12	Mark 15:1-24	Numbers 3	Psalm 26
13	Mark 15:25-47	Numbers 4	Psalm 27
14	Mark 16	Numbers 5-6	Psalm 28
15	Luke 1:1-25	Numbers 7	Psalm 29
16	Luke 1:26-56	Numbers 8-9	Psalm 30
17	Luke 1:57-80	Numbers 10	Psalm 31:1-13
18	Luke 2:1-24	Numbers 11	Psalm 31:14-24
19	Luke 2:25-52	Numbers 12-13	Psalm 32
20	Luke 3	Numbers 14	Psalm 33:1-11
21	Luke 4:1-30	Numbers 15	Psalm 33:12-22
22	Luke 4:31-44	Numbers 16	Psalm 34:1-10
23	Luke 5	Numbers 17-18	Psalm 34:11-22
24	Luke 6:1-26	Numbers 19-20	Psalm 35:1-16
25	Luke 6:27-49	Numbers 21	Psalm 35:17-28
26	Luke 7:1-23	Numbers 22	Psalm 36
27	Luke 7:24-50	Numbers 23-25	Psalm 37:1-20
28	Luke 8:1-25	Numbers 26	Psalm 37:21-40
29	Luke 8:26-56	Numbers 27-28	Psalm 38:1-12
30	Luke 9:1-36	Numbers 29-30	Psalm 38:13-22
31	Luke 9:37-62	Numbers 31	Psalm 39

Daily Bible Reading Schedule

APRIL			
Day	New Testament	Old Testament (a.m.)	Old Testament (p.m.)
1	Luke 10:1-22	Numbers 32	Psalm 40
2	Luke 10:23-42	Numbers 33-34	Psalm 41
3	Luke 11:1-28	Numbers 35-36	Psalm 42
4	Luke 11:29-54	Deuteronomy 1	Psalm 43
5	Luke 12:1-34	Deuteronomy 2-3	Psalm 44:1-14
6	Luke 12:35-59	Deuteronomy 4	Psalm 44:15-26
7	Luke 13	Deuteronomy 5-6	Psalm 45
8	Luke 14	Deuteronomy 7-8	Psalm 46
9	Luke 15	Deuteronomy 9-10	Psalm 47
10	Luke 16	Deuteronomy 11-12	Psalm 48
11	Luke 17	Deuteronomy 13-14	Psalm 49
12	Luke 18:1-17	Deuteronomy 15-16	Psalm 50
13	Luke 18:18-43	Deuteronomy 17-18	Psalm 51
14	Luke 19:1-27	Deuteronomy 19-21	Psalm 52
15	Luke 19:28-48	Deuteronomy 22-23	Psalm 53
16	Luke 20:1-26	Deuteronomy 24-25	Psalm 54
17	Luke 20:27-47	Deuteronomy 26-27	Psalm 55:1-11
18	Luke 21	Deuteronomy 28	Psalm 55:12-23
19	Luke 22:1-23	Deuteronomy 29-30	Psalm 56
20	Luke 22:24-46	Deuteronomy 31	Psalm 57
21	Luke 22:47-71	Deuteronomy 32	Psalm 58
22	Luke 23:1-26	Deuteronomy 33-34	Psalm 59
23	Luke 23:27-56	Joshua 1-2	Psalm 60
24	Luke 24:1-27	Joshua 3-5	Psalm 61
25	Luke 24:28-53	Joshua 6-7	Psalm 62
26	John 1:1-27	Joshua 8-9	Psalm 63
27	John 1:28-51	Joshua 10	Psalm 64
28	John 2	Joshua 11-12	Psalm 65
29	John 3	Joshua 13-14	Psalm 66
30	John 4:1-26	Joshua 15-16	Psalm 67

Daily Bible Reading Schedule

MAY			
Day	New Testament	Old Testament (a.m.)	Old Testament (p.m.)
1	John 4:27-54	Joshua 17-18	Psalm 68:1-18
2	John 5:1-23	Joshua 19	Psalm 68:19-35
3	John 5:24-47	Joshua 20-21	Psalm 69:1-18
4	John 6:1-21	Joshua 22-23	Psalm 69:19-36
5	John 6:22-48	Joshua 24	Psalm 70
6	John 6:49-71	Judges 1-2	Psalm 71:1-13
7	John 7:1-27	Judges 3-4	Psalm 71:14-24
8	John 7:28-53	Judges 5-6	Psalm 72
9	John 8:1-20	Judges 7-8	Psalm 73:1-15
10	John 8:21-40	Judges 9	Psalm 73:16-28
11	John 8:41-59	Judges 10-11	Psalm 74
12	John 9:1-23	Judges 12-14	Psalm 75
13	John 9:24-41	Judges 15-16	Psalm 76
14	John 10:1-21	Judges 17-18	Psalm 77
15	John 10:22-42	Judges 19	Psalm 78:1-18
16	John 11:1-29	Judges 20	Psalm 78:19-36
17	John 11:30-57	Judges 21	Psalm 78:37-54
18	John 12:1-26	Ruth 1-2	Psalm 78:55-72
19	John 12:27-50	Ruth 3-4	Psalm 79
20	John 13:1-20	I Samuel 1-2	Psalm 80
21	John 13:21-38	I Samuel 3-4	Psalm 81
22	John 14	I Samuel 5-7	Psalm 82
23	John 15	I Samuel 8-9	Psalm 83
24	John 16:1-16	I Samuel 10-11	Psalm 84
25	John 16:17-33	I Samuel 12-13	Psalm 85
26	John 17	I Samuel 14	Psalm 86
27	John 18:1-18	I Samuel 15-16	Psalm 87
28	John 18:19-40	I Samuel 17	Psalm 88
29	John 19:1-22	I Samuel 18-19	Psalm 89:1-17
30	John 19:23-42	I Samuel 20-21	Psalm 89:18-34
31	John 20	I Samuel 22-23	Psalm 89:35-52

Daily Bible Reading Schedule

Day	New Testament	Old Testament (a.m.)	Old Testament (p.m.)
JUNE			
1	John 21	I Samuel 24-25	Psalm 90
2	Acts 1	I Samuel 26-27	Psalm 91
3	Acts 2:1-21	I Samuel 28-29	Psalm 92
4	Acts 2:22-47	I Samuel 30-31	Psalm 93
5	Acts 3	II Samuel 1-2	Psalm 94:1-11
6	Acts 4:1-20	II Samuel 3-4	Psalm 94:12-23
7	Acts 4:21-37	II Samuel 5-6	Psalm 95
8	Acts 5:1-20	II Samuel 7-9	Psalm 96
9	Acts 5:21-42	II Samuel 10-11	Psalm 97
10	Acts 6	II Samuel 12-13	Psalm 98
11	Acts 7:1-19	II Samuel 14-15	Psalm 99
12	Acts 7:20-40	II Samuel 16-17	Psalm 100
13	Acts 7:41-60	II Samuel 18	Psalm 101
14	Acts 8:1-25	II Samuel 19	Psalm 102:1-11
15	Acts 8:26-40	II Samuel 20-21	Psalm 102:12-28
16	Acts 9:1-21	II Samuel 22	Psalm 103:1-12
17	Acts 9:22-43	II Samuel 23-24	Psalm 103:13-22
18	Acts 10:1-22	I Kings 1	Psalm 104:1-18
19	Acts 10:23-48	I Kings 2	Psalm 104:19-35
20	Acts 11	I Kings 3-4	Psalm 105:1-15
21	Acts 12	I Kings 5-6	Psalm 105:16-30
22	Acts 13:1-25	I Kings 7	Psalm 105:31-45
23	Acts 13:26-52	I Kings 8	Psalm 106:1-15
24	Acts 14	I Kings 9-10	Psalm 106:16-31
25	Acts 15:1-21	I Kings 11	Psalm 106:32-48
26	Acts 15:22-41	I Kings 12-13	Psalm 107:1-16
27	Acts 16:1-21	I Kings 14-15	Psalm 107:17-30
28	Acts 16:22-40	I Kings 16-17	Psalm 107:31-43
29	Acts 17:1-17	I Kings 18	Psalm 108
30	Acts 17:18-34	I Kings 19-20	Psalm 109:1-16

Daily Bible Reading Schedule

JULY			
Day	New Testament	Old Testament (a.m.)	Old Testament (p.m.)
1	Acts 18:1-17	I Kings 21	Psalm 109:17-31
2	Acts 18:18-28	I Kings 22	Psalm 110
3	Acts 19:1-20	II Kings 1-2	Psalm 111
4	Acts 19:21-41	II Kings 3-4	Psalm 112
5	Acts 20:1-16	II Kings 5-6	Psalm 113
6	Acts 20:17-38	II Kings 7-8	Psalm 114
7	Acts 21:1-17	II Kings 9	Psalm 115
8	Acts 21:18-40	II Kings 10	Psalm 116
9	Acts 22	II Kings 11-12	Psalm 117
10	Acts 23	II Kings 13-14	Psalm 118:1-14
11	Acts 24	II Kings 15	Psalm 118:15-29
12	Acts 25	II Kings 16-17	Psalm 119:1-8
13	Acts 26	II Kings 18	Psalm 119:9-16
14	Acts 27:1-25	II Kings 19-20	Psalm 119:17-24
15	Acts 27:26-44	II Kings 21-22	Psalm 119:25-32
16	Acts 28:1-16	II Kings 23	Psalm 119:33-40
17	Acts 28:17-31	II Kings 24-25	Psalm 119:41-48
18	Romans 1:1-17	I Chronicles 1-2	Psalm 119:49-56
19	Romans 1:18-32	I Chronicles 3-4	Psalm 119:57-64
20	Romans 2	I Chronicles 5	Psalm 119:65-72
21	Romans 3:1-18	I Chronicles 6	Psalm 119:73-80
22	Romans 3:19-31	I Chronicles 7-8	Psalm 119:81-88
23	Romans 4	I Chronicles 9-10	Psalm 119:89-96
24	Romans 5	I Chronicles 11	Psalm 119:97-104
25	Romans 6	I Chronicles 12-13	Psalm 119:105-112
26	Romans 7	I Chronicles 14-15	Psalm 119:113-120
27	Romans 8:1-18	I Chronicles 16	Psalm 119:121-128
28	Romans 8:19-39	I Chronicles 17-18	Psalm 119:129-136
29	Romans 9:1-16	I Chronicles 19-21	Psalm 119:137-144
30	Romans 9:17-33	I Chronicles 22-23	Psalm 119:145-152
31	Romans 10	I Chronicles 24-25	Psalm 119:153-160

Daily Bible Reading Schedule

AUGUST			
Day	New Testament	Old Testament (a.m.)	Old Testament (p.m.)
1	Romans 11:1-16	I Chronicles 26-27	Psalm 119:161-168
2	Romans 11:17-36	I Chronicles 28-29	Psalm 119:169-176
3	Romans 12	II Chronicles 1-2	Psalm 120
4	Romans 13	II Chronicles 3-5	Psalm 121
5	Romans 14	II Chronicles 6	Psalm 122
6	Romans 15:1-16	II Chronicles 7-8	Psalm 123
7	Romans 15:17-33	II Chronicles 9-10	Psalm 124
8	Romans 16	II Chronicles 11-12	Psalm 125
9	I Corinthians 1	II Chronicles 13-14	Psalm 126
10	I Corinthians 2	II Chronicles 15-17	Psalm 127
11	I Corinthians 3	II Chronicles 18-19	Psalm 128
12	I Corinthians 4	II Chronicles 20	Psalm 129
13	I Corinthians 5	II Chronicles 21-22	Psalm 130
14	I Corinthians 6	II Chronicles 23-24	Psalm 131
15	I Corinthians 7:1-20	II Chronicles 25-26	Psalm 132
16	I Corinthians 7:21-40	II Chronicles 27-28	Psalm 133
17	I Corinthians 8	II Chronicles 29	Psalm 134
18	I Corinthians 9	II Chronicles 30-31	Psalm 135
19	I Corinthians 10:1-17	II Chronicles 32	Psalm 136
20	I Corinthians 10:18-33	II Chronicles 33-34	Psalm 137
21	I Corinthians 11:1-16	II Chronicles 35-36	Psalm 138
22	I Corinthians 11:17-34	Ezra 1-2	Psalm 139:1-13
23	I Corinthians 12:1-13	Ezra 3-5	Psalm 139:14-24
24	I Corinthians 12:14-31	Ezra 6-7	Psalm 140
25	I Corinthians 13	Ezra 8-9	Psalm 141
26	I Corinthians 14:1-20	Ezra 10	Psalm 142
27	I Corinthians 14:21-40	Nehemiah 1-2	Psalm 143
28	I Corinthians 15:1-20	Nehemiah 3-4	Psalm 144
29	I Corinthians 15:21-40	Nehemiah 5-6	Psalm 145
30	I Corinthians 15:41-58	Nehemiah 7-8	Psalm 146
31	I Corinthians 16	Nehemiah 9	Psalm 147:1-11

Daily Bible Reading Schedule

SEPTEMBER			
Day	New Testament	Old Testament (a.m.)	Old Testament (p.m.)
1	II Corinthians 1	Nehemiah 10-11	Psalm 147:12-20
2	II Corinthians 2	Nehemiah 12	Psalm 148
3	II Corinthians 3	Nehemiah 13	Psalm 149
4	II Corinthians 4	Esther 1-3	Psalm 150
5	II Corinthians 5	Esther 4-7	Proverbs 1:1-9
6	II Corinthians 6	Esther 8-10	Proverbs 1:10-19
7	II Corinthians 7	Isaiah 1-2	Proverbs 1:20-33
8	II Corinthians 8	Isaiah 3-5	Proverbs 2:1-11
9	II Corinthians 9	Isaiah 6-8	Proverbs 2:12-22
10	II Corinthians 10	Isaiah 9-10	Proverbs 3:1-10
11	II Corinthians 11:1-15	Isaiah 11-13	Proverbs 3:11-24
12	II Corinthians 11:16-33	Isaiah 14-16	Proverbs 3:25-35
13	II Corinthians 12	Isaiah 17-20	Proverbs 4:1-13
14	II Corinthians 13	Isaiah 21-23	Proverbs 4:14-27
15	Galatians 1	Isaiah 24-26	Proverbs 5:1-14
16	Galatians 2	Isaiah 27-29	Proverbs 5:15-23
17	Galatians 3	Isaiah 30-32	Proverbs 6:1-11
18	Galatians 4:1-16	Isaiah 33-35	Proverbs 6:12-22
19	Galatians 4:17-31	Isaiah 36-37	Proverbs 6:23-35
20	Galatians 5	Isaiah 38-40	Proverbs 7:1-12
21	Galatians 6	Isaiah 41-42	Proverbs 7:13-27
22	Ephesians 1	Isaiah 43-44	Proverbs 8:1-18
23	Ephesians 2	Isaiah 45-47	Proverbs 8:19-36
24	Ephesians 3	Isaiah 48-49	Proverbs 9:1-9
25	Ephesians 4:1-16	Isaiah 50-52	Proverbs 9:10-18
26	Ephesians 4:17-32	Isaiah 53-56	Proverbs 10:1-11
27	Ephesians 5:1-17	Isaiah 57-59	Proverbs 10:12-22
28	Ephesians 5:18-33	Isaiah 60-62	Proverbs 10:23-32
29	Ephesians 6	Isaiah 63-64	Proverbs 11:1-10
30	Philippians 1:1-14	Isaiah 65-66	Proverbs 11:11-20

Daily Bible Reading Schedule

OCTOBER			
Day	New Testament	Old Testament (a.m.)	Old Testament (p.m.)
1	Philippians 1:15-30	Jeremiah 1-2	Proverbs 11:21-31
2	Philippians 2:1-16	Jeremiah 3-4	Proverbs 12:1-10
3	Philippians 2:17-30	Jeremiah 5-6	Proverbs 12:11-19
4	Philippians 3	Jeremiah 7-8	Proverbs 12:20-28
5	Philippians 4	Jeremiah 9-10	Proverbs 13:1-8
6	Colossians 1	Jeremiah 11-12	Proverbs 13:9-17
7	Colossians 2	Jeremiah 13-14	Proverbs 13:18-25
8	Colossians 3	Jeremiah 15-16	Proverbs 14:1-11
9	Colossians 4	Jeremiah 17-18	Proverbs 14:12-23
10	I Thessalonians 1	Jeremiah 19-20	Proverbs 14:24-35
11	I Thessalonians 2	Jeremiah 21-22	Proverbs 15:1-11
12	I Thessalonians 3	Jeremiah 23	Proverbs 15:12-22
13	I Thessalonians 4	Jeremiah 24-25	Proverbs 15:23-33
14	I Thessalonians 5	Jeremiah 26-27	Proverbs 16:1-11
15	II Thessalonians 1	Jeremiah 28-29	Proverbs 16:12-22
16	II Thessalonians 2	Jeremiah 30-31	Proverbs 16:23-33
17	II Thessalonians 3	Jeremiah 32	Proverbs 17:1-9
18	I Timothy 1	Jeremiah 33-34	Proverbs 17:10-18
19	I Timothy 2	Jeremiah 35-36	Proverbs 17:19-28
20	I Timothy 3	Jeremiah 37-38	Proverbs 18:1-8
21	I Timothy 4	Jeremiah 39-40	Proverbs 18:9-16
22	I Timothy 5	Jeremiah 41-42	Proverbs 18:17-24
23	I Timothy 6	Jeremiah 43-44	Proverbs 19:1-9
24	II Timothy 1	Jeremiah 45-47	Proverbs 19:10-19
25	II Timothy 2	Jeremiah 48	Proverbs 19:20-29
26	II Timothy 3	Jeremiah 49	Proverbs 20:1-10
27	II Timothy 4	Jeremiah 50	Proverbs 20:11-20
28	Titus 1	Jeremiah 51	Proverbs 20:21-30
29	Titus 2	Jeremiah 52	Proverbs 21:1-10
30	Titus 3	Lamentations 1-2	Proverbs 21:11-20
31	Philemon	Lamentations 3	Proverbs 21:21-31

Daily Bible Reading Schedule

Day	New Testament	Old Testament (a.m.)	Old Testament (p.m.)
NOVEMBER				

Day	New Testament	Old Testament (a.m.)	Old Testament (p.m.)
1	Hebrews 1	Lamentations 4-5	Proverbs 22:1-9
2	Hebrews 2	Ezekiel 1-2	Proverbs 22:10-19
3	Hebrews 3	Ezekiel 3-4	Proverbs 22:20-29
4	Hebrews 4	Ezekiel 5-6	Proverbs 23:1-12
5	Hebrews 5	Ezekiel 7-8	Proverbs 23:13-23
6	Hebrews 6	Ezekiel 9-10	Proverbs 23:24-35
7	Hebrews 7	Ezekiel 11-12	Proverbs 24:1-9
8	Hebrews 8	Ezekiel 13-15	Proverbs 24:10-18
9	Hebrews 9	Ezekiel 16	Proverbs 24:19-26
10	Hebrews 10:1-18	Ezekiel 17-18	Proverbs 24:27-34
11	Hebrews 10:19-39	Ezekiel 19-20	Proverbs 25:1-7
12	Hebrews 11:1-20	Ezekiel 21-22	Proverbs 25:8-14
13	Hebrews 11:21-40	Ezekiel 23	Proverbs 25:15-20
14	Hebrews 12	Ezekiel 24-25	Proverbs 25:21-28
15	Hebrews 13	Ezekiel 26-27	Proverbs 26:1-7
16	James 1	Ezekiel 28-29	Proverbs 26:8-12
17	James 2	Ezekiel 30-31	Proverbs 26:13-19
18	James 3	Ezekiel 32-33	Proverbs 26:20-28
19	James 4	Ezekiel 34-35	Proverbs 27:1-7
20	James 5	Ezekiel 36-37	Proverbs 27:8-14
21	I Peter 1	Ezekiel 38-39	Proverbs 27:15-21
22	I Peter 2	Ezekiel 40	Proverbs 27:22-27
23	I Peter 3	Ezekiel 41-42	Proverbs 28:1-7
24	I Peter 4	Ezekiel 43-44	Proverbs 28:8-14
25	I Peter 5	Ezekiel 45-46	Proverbs 28:15-21
26	II Peter 1	Ezekiel 47-48	Proverbs 28:22-28
27	II Peter 2	Daniel 1	Proverbs 29:1-7
28	II Peter 3	Daniel 2	Proverbs 29:8-14
29	I John 1	Daniel 3	Proverbs 29:15-21
30	I John 2:1-14	Daniel 4	Proverbs 29:22-27

Daily Bible Reading Schedule

Day	New Testament	Old Testament (a.m.)	Old Testament (p.m.)
DECEMBER			
1	I John 2:15-29	Daniel 5-6	Proverbs 30:1-9
2	I John 3	Daniel 7-8	Proverbs 30:10-16
3	I John 4	Daniel 9-10	Proverbs 30:17-23
4	I John 5	Daniel 11-12	Proverbs 30:24-33
5	II John	Hosea 1-2	Proverbs 31:1-9
6	III John	Hosea 3-5	Proverbs 31:10-16
7	Jude	Hosea 6-8	Proverbs 31:17-23
8	Revelation 1	Hosea 9-11	Proverbs 31:24-31
9	Revelation 2:1-17	Hosea 12-14	Ecclesiastes 1
10	Revelation 2:18-29	Joel 1-2	Ecclesiastes 2:1-11
11	Revelation 3	Joel 3	Ecclesiastes 2:12-26
12	Revelation 4	Amos 1-3	Ecclesiastes 3:1-11
13	Revelation 5	Amos 4-6	Ecclesiastes 3:12-22
14	Revelation 6	Amos 7-9	Ecclesiastes 4
15	Revelation 7	Obadiah	Ecclesiastes 5
16	Revelation 8	Jonah 1-4	Ecclesiastes 6
17	Revelation 9	Micah 1-3	Ecclesiastes 7:1-15
18	Revelation 10	Micah 4-5	Ecclesiastes 7:16-29
19	Revelation 11	Micah 6-7	Ecclesiastes 8
20	Revelation 12	Nahum 1-3	Ecclesiastes 9
21	Revelation 13	Habakkuk 1-3	Ecclesiastes 10
22	Revelation 14	Zephaniah 1-3	Ecclesiastes 11
23	Revelation 15	Haggai 1-2	Ecclesiastes 12
24	Revelation 16	Zechariah 1-2	Song of Solomon 1
25	Matthew 1, Luke 2	Zechariah 3-5	Song of Solomon 2
26	Revelation 17	Zechariah 6-8	Song of Solomon 3
27	Revelation 18	Zechariah 9-10	Song of Solomon 4
28	Revelation 19	Zechariah 11-12	Song of Solomon 5
29	Revelation 20	Zechariah 13-14	Song of Solomon 6
30	Revelation 21	Malachi 1-2	Song of Solomon 7
31	Revelation 22	Malachi 3-4	Song of Solomon 8

Where to Look in the Bible

ADDICTION I Corinthians 6:12, I Peter 2:11, Hebrews 12:1, I Corinthians 9:27, II Corinthians 10:3-5

ADULTERY Hebrews 13:4, James 4:4, Proverbs 6:32, Matthew 5:28, Exodus 20:14, Luke 16:18, Matthew 5:32 & 19:9, Mark 10:11-12, I Corinthians 6:13 & 6:18, Galatians 5:19, Ephesians 5:3, I Thessalonians 4:3

ANGER Psalm 30:5, Ecclesiastes 7:9, Psalm 7:11, Proverbs 14:17 & 14:29, Ephesians 4:26-27, Proverbs 29:22, Proverbs 19:19, James 1:19-20, Psalm 37:8, Proverbs 16:32, Psalm 103:8, Proverbs 15:1, Colossians 3:8 & 3:21, Psalm 30:5

BELIEVE Mark 1:5, Mark 9:23-24, Romans 10:9, Luke 24:25, John 1:12, John 8:24, John 14:1, Acts 16:31, Ephesians 1:13, John 5:24 & 6:29 & 6:47, Acts 10:43 & 13:39 & 27:25, Romans 1:16, Mark 11:24, I John 5:5 & 5:13

BIBLE Psalm 12:6-7, Psalm 119:105, Psalm 119:140, II Timothy 3:16-17, II Peter 1:19-21, Deuteronomy 6:6, Hebrews 4:12, Ephesians 6:17, John 15:3, Proverbs 30:5-6, Revelation 22:19

BITTERNESS Colossians 3:19, James 3:14, Ephesians 4:31, Hebrews 12:15

BOLDNESS Philippians 1:14, Hebrews 4:16, Ephesians 3:12, Proverbs 28:1, Acts 4:13 & 4:29 & 4:31, Hebrews 10:19, I John 4:17

BURDEN Psalm 55:22, Matthew 11:29-30, Galatians 6:2 & 6:5, Psalm 38:4, Acts 15:28, II Corinthians 12:16

CARNAL	Romans 7:14, Romans 8:6-7, I Corinthians 3:1, II Corinthians 10:4
CHASTENING	Psalm 6:1, Proverbs 19:18, Daniel 10:12, Revelation 3:19, Psalm 118:18, Hebrews 12:5-10, Psalm 94:12, Proverbs 3:11
CHILDREN	Matthew 18:1 & 19:14, Luke 9:48, Luke 18:17, John 13:33, Proverbs 13:24 & 20:11 & 22:6 & 22:15 & 23:13-14 & 29:15, Ephesians 6:1-4, Colossians 3:20-21
CLEAN	John 15:3, Proverbs 16:2, Isaiah 1:16, John 13:11, Psalm 19:12 & 24:4 & 51:10 & 119:9, James 4:8, Jeremiah 33:8, II Corinthians 7:1, I John 1:7
COMFORT	Matthew 9:22, Acts 9:31, II Corinthians 1:4 & 7:4, Psalm 23:4, I Thessalonians 4:18, John 14:18
CONFIDENCE	Proverbs 3:26 & 14:26, Ephesians 3:12, Psalm 118:8, Philippians 3:3, I John 5:14-15, Acts 28:31, II Corinthians 7:16, Hebrews 10:35, II Thessalonians 3:4
CONTENTMENT AND SATISFACTION	Psalm 63:5-6, John 4:13-14, Psalm 103:5, Psalm 107:9, Psalm 37:4, Matthew 5:6, Philippians 4:11, Matthew 6:33
CULTURE	Matthew 15:3, Mark 7:8-9, Colossians 2:8, Titus 1:14, I Peter 1:18, I John 2:15
DEBT	Psalm 37:21, Proverbs 22:7, Proverbs 22:26-27, Deuteronomy 28:12
DISCOURAGE-MENT	I Samuel 30:6, Psalm 31:24, Psalm 138:7, John 14:1, Hebrews 10:35-36, Isaiah 51:11, Philippians 4:6-7, II Corinthians 4:8-9, John 14:27, Psalm 27:1-14, Deuteronomy 1:21 & 3:28, Colossians 3:21, Psalm 121:1, I Chronicles 16:27, Psalm 51:8, Acts 27:25, I Thessalonians 5:18, I Peter 1:6-7

DOUBT	Romans 10:17, Isaiah 59:1, I Thessalonians 5:24, Mark 11:22-24, Romans 4:20-21, Luke 12:29-31, II Peter 3:9, Matthew 14:31, Matthew 21:21, Romans 14:23, I Timothy 2:8
DRINKING	Proverbs 20:1, Proverbs 21:17, Proverbs 23:29-31, Isaiah 5:11, Ephesians 5:18, Habakkuk 2:5
EMPLOYEES	Proverbs 17:2, Proverbs 25:13, Proverbs 27:18, Ephesians 6:5, Colossians 3:22, Titus 2:9, I Peter 2:18, I Timothy 6:1
EMPLOYERS	Deuteronomy 24:15, Ephesians 6:9, Colossians 4:1, Jeremiah 22:13, James 5:4, Exodus 1:13
FAITH	II Corinthians 5:7, I Peter 1:7, Matthew 17:20, Romans 10:17, Hebrews 11:1 & 6, Matthew 9:28-29, Mark 11:22-24, Hebrews 12:2-3, Mark 9:23, Matthew 9:20-22
FAMILY PROBLEMS	Joshua 24:15, Romans 13:10, Ephesians 5:21-33, Ephesians 4:31-32, I Peter 3:1-7, Proverbs 10:12, Genesis 2:18, Proverbs 13:10, I Peter 1:22, Genesis 2:24, Psalm 101:2, I Peter 3:8-11, Colossians 3:19
FEAR	II Timothy 1:7, Psalm 56:3, Deuteronomy 31:8, Joshua 1:9, Luke 1:74, I John 4:18, Genesis 15:11, Deuteronomy 1:21, Deuteronomy 20:3, Joshua 10:25, Judges 6:23, I Samuel 12:20, II Kings 6:16, I Chronicles 28:20, Isaiah 35:4, Isaiah 41:13, Isaiah 43:1, Daniel 10:19, Joel 2:21, Zechariah 8:13, Matthew 10:28, Luke 8:50
FORGIVENESS	Psalm 85:2, Hebrews 8:12, Psalm 103:12, Psalm 32:1-2, Isaiah 43:25, I John 2:1, Ephesians 1:7, Mark 11:25, Isaiah 55:7, Proverbs 28:13, I John 1:7 & 9

FRIENDS	Psalm 119:63; Proverbs 17:9, 17; Proverbs 18:24; Proverbs 27:6, 9, 17, 19; Amos 3:3; John 15:13
GIVING	Malachi 3:8-11, Matthew 6:1-4, Luke 6:38, Luke 21:4, I Corinthians 16:2, Proverbs 3:9, Proverbs 11:24-25, Proverbs 28:27, Acts 20:35, II Corinthians 8:1-5, II Corinthians 9:6-7
GRACE	II Corinthians 9:8, II Corinthians 12:9, James 4:6, Romans 16:20, I Corinthians 15:10, I Peter 5:5, II Peter 3:18, Hebrews 4:16, II Timothy 2:1, Titus 2:11-12, Hebrews 12:28, Acts 4:33, Psalm 84:11, Exodus 33:17, Philemon 1:25, I Timothy 1:14, Colossians 3:16, Colossians 4:6, Ephesians 3:8, II Corinthians 13:14, John 1:14
GUIDANCE AND WISDOM	Psalm 48:14, Psalm 37:5, Proverbs 16:3, James 1:5, Proverbs 1:7, Proverbs 2:6, Proverbs 3:5-6, Proverbs 24:5
HAPPINESS	Proverbs 16:20, Psalm 144:15, Proverbs 28:14, Proverbs 29:18, John 13:17, Job 5:17, James 5:11, I Peter 3:14, I Peter 4:14
HEAVEN	John 14:1-6, Luke 10:20, II Corinthians 5:1, Colossians 1:5, Revelation 22:14, Revelation 21:1-27, II Corinthians 5:8
HELL	Matthew 5:22, Matthew 18:9, Mark 9:43-48, Luke 12:5, II Peter 2:4, Luke 16:19-31
HELP IN TROUBLE	Philippians 4:9-13, II Corinthians 3:5, II Corinthians 12:9, Romans 8:28, II Peter 1:4, Romans 8:32, Psalm 55:22, Psalm 54:7, Psalm 50:15, Psalm 46:1, Psalm 40:13-17, Psalm 34:6-7, Psalm 34:18-19, Psalm 3:6, Psalm 4:8, Psalm 138:7, Psalm 145:18, Psalm 121:1-2, Isaiah 43:2, Psalm 31:7, I Peter 5:7, Hebrews 4:16

HELP THROUGH PRAYER	Matthew 21:22, Mark 11:24, I John 3:22, Philippians 4:19, John 16:24, Philippians 4:13, John 15:7, Psalm 68:19, Ephesians 3:20-21, Jeremiah 33:3, Jeremiah 32:17, Luke 1:37
HOLY SPIRIT	John 14:16-17, Luke 11:13, Ephesians 5:18, I Corinthians 6:19, John 16:7 & 13, Acts 1:8 & 4:31, Romans 5:5, John 7:38-39, Matthew 3:11
HUSBANDS	Genesis 2:24, Proverbs 5:18, Ecclesiastes 9:9, I Corinthians 7:3, I Corinthians 7:11, Ephesians 5:25, I Peter 3:7
JESUS IS GOD	Titus 2:13, Matthew 1:23, Revelation 17:14, Matthew 12:8, Acts 10:36, John 1:1-14, Acts 20:28, Colossians 1:16, Colossian 2:9, Hebrews 1:3, I John 5:7, I John 5:20, I Timothy 3:16, John 5:18, John 10:30-33, John 12:45, John 20:28, Hebrews 1:8
JOY	Psalm 43:4, Proverbs 28:14, Romans 15:13, Isaiah 55:12, Psalm 16:11, Psalm 51:8-12, Psalm 126:5, Luke 15:7, John 15:11, John 16:20-22, Acts 20:24, Galatians 5:22, James 1:2, I Peter 1:8, I Thessalonians 5:16, Philippians 4:4, Acts 5:41
LAZINESS	Proverbs 6:6, Proverbs 12:27, Proverbs 13:4, Proverbs 18:9, Proverbs 20:4, Hebrews 6:12, Romans 12:11, II Thessalonians 3:10-12
LONELINESS	Psalm 27:10, Psalm 46:1, Hebrews 13:5, Isaiah 41:10, Matthew 28:20, I Peter 5:7, Romans 8:35-39, Isaiah 54:10, Deuteronomy 4:31, Psalm 147:3, John 14:18, Isaiah 43:2, Joshua 1:5, Deuteronomy 31:6
LOVE	Proverbs 8:17, I John 4:16-21, Romans 5:8, John 15:9-13, I Corinthians 13, Psalm 42:8, I Peter 1:22, Hebrews 13:1, I John 3:18, Luke 6:27, John 14:15

LUST	Proverbs 6:25, Matthew 5:28, Galatians 5:16, II Timothy 2:22, James 1:14-15, I Peter 2:11, I Corinthians 10:6, II Peter 1:4, I John 2:16-17
LYING	Ephesians 4:25; Psalm 31:18, 119:29, 119:163; John 8:44; Proverbs 6:16-17, 12:19, 12:22, 13:5, 17:7, 21:6, 26:28
MODESTY	Deuteronomy 22:5, I Timothy 2:9-10, I Peter 3:1-6, Proverbs 7:10, Proverbs 31:30
MONEY PROBLEMS	Psalm 23:1, Luke 6:38, Malachi 3:10-12, Matthew 6:31-33, Joshua 1:8, Deuteronomy 28:2-8, II Corinthians 9:6-8, Philippians 4:19, Psalm 37:25, Psalm 24:10
MUSIC	Ephesians 5:19, Colossians 3:16, Hebrews 2:12, Psalm 40:3, Psalm 33:1-4, I Peter 2:11, Mark 14:26, Acts 16:25
OBEDIENCE	Ephesians 6:1-3, Deuteronomy 11:26-28, Acts 5:29, Hebrews 13:17, John 13:17, I Samuel 15:22, Isaiah 1:19, Jeremiah 7:23, Galatians 5:7, Romans 6:16, Colossians 3:22, II Thessalonians 3:14
ONCE SAVED ALWAYS SAVED	Romans 8:38-39, John 6:27 & 6:37, John 10:27-29, Philippians 1:6, I Peter 1:3-5, Jude 24-25, II Thessalonians 3:3, Psalm 23:6, Ephesians 4:30, Ephesians 1:13, II Timothy 2:13, II Corinthians 1:22, I Corinthians 1:9, II Thessalonians 2:16
PATIENCE	Psalm 130:5, Psalm 33:20, Psalm 27:14, Psalm 62:5, Psalm 145:15-16, Isaiah 40:31, Lamentations 3:22-26
PRIDE	Psalm 10:4, 12:3, 138:6; Proverbs 6:16-17, 11:2, 13:10, 15:25, 16:5, 16:18, 29:23; Daniel 4:37; James 4:6; I Peter 5:5; I John 2:16

SATAN	II Corinthians 2:11, II Corinthians 11:14, I John 3:10, Revelation 20:10, James 4:7, I Peter 5:8, John 8:44, Ephesians 2:2
SEPARATION	Ephesians 5:11, II Corinthians 6:14-18, Isaiah 52:11, Psalm 101:3-5, I John 2:15-16, II Thessalonians 3:6 & 14, I Corinthians 5:11, Romans 16:17-18
SERVING GOD	Romans 12:1-2 & 10-13, Matthew 6:24, Exodus 23:25-26, Deuteronomy 13:4, Psalm 100:2, Deuteronomy 10:12, Joshua 22:25, Psalm 2:11, Joshua 24:14-18, Colossians 3:24
SLEEP	Psalm 3:5, 4:8, 127:2; Proverbs 3:24, 6:9-11, 10:5, 20:13; Matthew 26:40
STRENGTH	Ephesians 6:10-13, Colossians 1:10-11, Isaiah 41:10, Daniel 10:19, Psalm 18:1-2, Psalm 40:31, Psalm 119:28, Psalm 27:1, Nehemiah 8:10, Isaiah 40:29, Ephesians 3:16-17, Philippians 4:13, Psalm 27:14, Psalm 138:3, Proverbs 28:1
SUBMITTING TO AUTHORITY	Hebrews 13:7 & 17, I Samuel 15:23, I Peter 2:13-15, Proverbs 14:16-17, I Peter 5:5-6, Isaiah 1:19-20
TEMPTATION	II Peter 2:9, Psalm 119:11, I Corinthians 10:12-13, Hebrews 4:14-16, I Peter 5:8-9, James 4:7, James 1:2-3, Ephesians 6:10-11, Romans 6:14, I John 4:4, James 1:12-14, I John 1:9, Matthew 26:41, Matthew 4:1-11
THANKFULNESS	Deuteronomy 8:10, Psalm 50:14, Psalm 100:4, Psalm 107:15, Psalm 119:62, Colossians 1:12, Colossians 2:7, Colossians 3:15, Colossians 4:2, Ephesians 5:4, Ephesians 5:20, Philippians 4:6, I Thessalonians 5:18, I Timothy 1:12, I Timothy 2:1, Hebrews 13:15
TIME	Psalm 90:12, Ephesians 5:15-16, Colossians 4:5, Proverbs 27:1, James 4:13-14, Psalm 31:15

TONGUE, THE	Psalm 34:13, Proverbs 13:3, Proverbs 21:23, James 1:26, I Peter 3:10, Psalm 141:3, Proverbs 17: 28, Proverbs 10:19, James 3:1-12
TONGUES	Acts 2:4-11, I Corinthians 12:30, I Corinthians 13:8, I Corinthians 14:26-40
VICTORY OVER SIN	I John 5:4, I Corinthians 15:57-58, Romans 8:1-13, I John 1:7-9, Psalm 119:9-10, Romans 6:11-13, II Corinthians 10:4-5 & 11:31-32, Galatians 2:20, Ephesians 4:22-23, Colossians 3:15, I Timothy 4:16, Romans 14:10
WIDOWS	Romans 7:3, I Timothy 3:5-6, I Corinthians 7:39, I Corinthians 7:8-9, Psalm 146:9, Proverbs 15:25
WIFE	Proverbs 31:10-31, I Corinthians 7:10, Ephesians 5:22-24, Colossians 3:18, Titus 2:3-5, I Peter 3:1, Genesis 2:18, Genesis 3:16, Psalm 128:3, I Corinthians 14:34-35, Proverbs 12:4, Proverbs 14:1, Proverbs 21:19
WITNESSING	Acts 1:8, Mark 16:15, Matthew 28:18-20, John 4:35, Romans 10:1, Proverbs 11:30, Psalm 126:5-6, Acts 4:31, Daniel 12:3
WITCHCRAFT	Exodus 22:18, Leviticus 19:31 & 20:6, Deuteronomy 18:10-11, II Kings 21:6, Galatians 5:20-21
WORK	I Thessalonians 4:11, II Thessalonians 3:10, Psalm 104:23, Proverbs 18:9, Proverbs 20:11, I Corinthians 15:58, Titus 3:14
WORLDLINESS	Luke 21:34, Romans 12:2, Colossians 3:2, Titus 2:12, James 4:4, I John 2:15, Ephesians 2:2, II Timothy 4:10, Exodus 23:2, Luke 9:25, Matthew 6:19, I Thessalonians 5:22, I Peter 2:11, Mark 4:19, I Corinthians 10:7, Romans 13:14, Galatians 5:24, Titus 3:3, I Peter 4:2

Dictionary of Uncommon Words in the King James Bible

This is, by no means, a comprehensive dictionary. It is to be used as a quick reference only and may not be as accurate as a proper Bible dictionary, which defines each word as found in the context of Scripture. Please note that some of the words in this dictionary have more than one meaning. It is impossible to give all of the possible meanings for any given word. However, an effort was made to provide the definitions that are not common. (For example, the word *seed* often refers to the substance used for planting, but *seed* also means descendants. Because "descendants" is not commonly used today, that definition is provided.)

abhorrest	detest, hate	**amiss**	wrong, improper
abide	remain	**anise**	dill (a spice)
abomination	disgusting, detestable	**anon**	immediately, at once, without delay
aboundeth	overflows greatly		
abroad	far and wide	**array**	military formation
accursed	under a curse		
admonition	warning	**ascend**	go up
adorning	clothing, attire	**asps**	poisonous snakes
adversary	enemy	**ass**	donkey
advocate	one who pleads our case	**assayed**	tried, attempted
		asswaged	decreased, subsided
affirm	declare firmly		
afore	before	**asunder**	apart, into pieces
aforetime	formerly	**atonement**	reconciliation
albeit	although, even though	**availeth**	profits, has power to accomplish
alienated	excluded		
alms	gifts to the poor	**backbiting**	slandering
altogether	entirely, totally	**bade**	invited, told
alway	always	**barbarians**	uncivilized, crude
amend	correct, improve	**barren**	unable to conceive; empty

base	lowest, common	**buffet**	strike with hand or fist
bear	carry	**bullock**	young bull
beckoned	signaled	**busybodies**	gossips, meddlers
beeves	plural of beef	**calamity**	deep trouble, disaster
begat	fathered		
beguiled	deceived, tricked	**canker**	anything that corrupts or causes decay
behold	look at		
bereave	deprive		
beseech	beg	**careful**	worried, concerned
besought	begged		
bestowed	given	**carefulness**	worry, concern
betimes	early, quickly	**carnal**	fleshly
betrothed	promised in marriage	**censer**	container in which incense is burned
betwixt	between		
bewail	mourn	**chambering**	sexual indulgence or lewdness
bewrayeth	reveals, betrays		
bishop	overseer		
blaspheme	to speak of God irreverently	**charge**	command
bondmaid	slave girl	**charity**	love; unselfish, self-sacrificing concern for others
bondman	male slave		
bonds	chains, shackles	**chasteneth**	correctively punishes
borne	carried		
bosom	chest	**chastise**	punish by beating
brawlers	noisy fighters, quarrelers	**circumspectly**	cautiously, carefully
breech	break	**clamour**	loud demand, complaint
brimstone	sulfur		
		cleave	cling, hold to
brutish	beast-like: stupid, cruel, crude	**comely**	beautiful
buckler	defense, protection	**commend**	entrust
		commendeth	exhibit, show
		communed	spoke

communicate	give, impart	**custom**	debt
compassed	surrounded	**dam**	mother of an animal
concord	agreement	**damnation**	condemnation
concubine	mistress	**damsel**	girl
concupiscence	strong desire or appetite, it also includes especially strong sexual desire	**daubed**	covered
		dayspring	daybreak, sun-rising
confound	confuse	**dearth**	famine, drought
consecrated	set apart	**deep, (the)**	the sea
consolation	comfort	**deferreth**	delays
constraineth	compels, forces	**defraud**	withhold
contemned	despised	**desolate**	deserted, barren
contemptible	utterly despised	**destitute**	lacking, empty
contentious	ready to argue, fond of strife or quarreling	**devils**	demons, evil spirits
		disannul	completely cancel
contrariwise	on the contrary	**discord**	conflict
convenient	appropriate, suitable, fitting	**disorderly**	in a lawless, unruly way
conversation	behavior, conduct	**dispensation**	administration
conies	small, rabbit-like animals	**disposed**	willing
		disputation	discussion, debate, argument
corn	grain	**dissembleth**	acts like a hypocrite, disguises
coupled	joined		
couplings	joiners, braces		
covert	shelter	**dissension**	strife
covetous	unsatisfied; desiring more	**dissimulation**	hypocrisy, deception
		divers	several
cumbrance	troublesome burden, hindrance	**divination**	predicting by magic or witchcraft
cunning	skillful, clever; sly	**dominion**	power, authority

doting	foolish or excessive fondness	**espoused**	promised in marriage, engaged
drave	drove	**esteem**	value
dumb	voiceless, cannot speak	**esteemeth**	considers
		eunuch	castrated man
dung	waste matter, manure	**eventide**	evening
durst	dared	**evermore**	always, continually
earnest	down payment	**exceedingly**	extremely, very
edify	build up	**exhortation**	encouragement
effectually	effectively	**expedient**	profitable, useful
effeminate	soft, a homosexual	**expounded**	explained
		extol	praise highly
elect	chosen	**extortion**	using threats for money
election	selection		
emboldened	made bold	**faint**	lose courage or hope
emulation	desire to equal or surpass another	**fair**	attractive, beautiful
enchantment	magic spells, or charms	**familiar spirit**	demon
endeavoured	earnestly tried	**feign**	pretend
enjoin	command, order	**fervent**	zealous
ensamples	examples	**fidelity**	faithfulness
enticing	alluring	**firmament**	sky
ephah	ancient Hebrew unit of dry measure (about 36 liters)	**firstlings**	firstborn ones
		fitly	properly
		forbear	abstain, stop, avoid
epistle	letter		
equity	fairness	**forbearance**	patience
ere	before		
err	do wrong	**forbearing**	refraining from, giving up
eschew	avoid, abstain from	**forasmuch**	because, since
		foreknowledge	forethought

fornication	sexual relations outside of marriage	**hailing**	pulling, hauling
forth	out	**hallowed**	set apart
forthwith	immediately, at once	**halt**	lame, crippled
forward	active, diligent	**handmaiden**	female servant
forwardness	zeal, eagerness	**haply**	perhaps
fourscore	80	**harlot**	prostitute, whore
foursquare	with four equal sides	**hast**	have
fowl	flying creatures	**hasteth**	hurries
fretteth	irritated	**havock**	great destruction
froward	crooked, warped, perverted, contrary	**heady**	willful, domineering
furious	violently angry	**hearken**	listen carefully
gainsaying	opposing, contradicting	**heed**	care, careful notice
garner	storehouse for grain	**heirs**	inheritors
gat	got	**help meet**	suitable helper
gender	produce	**hence**	from here, away
ghost	spirit	**henceforth**	from now on
girdles	belts	**hereafter**	after this
girt	fasten(ed)	**hereby**	by this
glean	collect	**herein**	in this
gleaning	leftovers	**hewn**	cut, chopped
glorying	boasting	**highminded**	proud, arrogant
gnashed	chewed (in pain or anger)	**hireling**	hired man
		hither	here
God speed	good success, "God bless you"	**hitherto**	until this time
		hoary	white or grayish
gravity	seriousness	**holden**	held
grievous	painful	**holpen**	helped
guile	deceit	**howbeit**	nevertheless
		ignominy	dishonor, shame
		immutable	unchangeable
		implacable	cannot be reconciled or appeased

impotent	not powerful, helpless, weak	laver	basin, bowl, or other vessel for washing
impudent	shameless	leaven	yeast
impute	to credit or put something on one's account	liberal	generous
		listeth	wishes, likes, chooses
incontinency	lack of self-control	loatheth	hates, feels intense dislike
incontinent	uncontrolled	loathsome	detestable, disgusting, nauseating
indignation	anger		
infidel	unbeliever		
infirmity	weakness	lusts	cravings, desires
injurious	harmful	malefactor	evildoer
innumerable	uncountable	malice	desire to harm others or to see others suffer
insomuch	to such a degree		
instant	earnest, urgent		
intreat	beg	maliciousness	evil
jot	a very small part	malignity	intense hatred and ill-will
jubilee	time of rejoicing or celebration	manifest	clearly revealed or shown
justified	declared or made righteous	manifold	much
keep	guard, protect	mar	disfigure, spoil
kindle	stir up, ignite	marvel	wonder
kindred	family	matrix	womb
kinswoman	female relative	mean men	men of low rank
knew	knew sexually	meet	fitting, suitable, proper
knop	knob, rounded lump for ornament		
		members	body parts
		mete	measure
laden	loaded, burdened	midst	middle
lament	mourn, grieve	mingled	mixed
languisheth	wastes away	mirth	joyfulness
lasciviousness	lustfulness	mischief	harm, injury, damage
latchet	strap or lace		
laud	praise, magnify		

molten	melted and molded	**preeminence**	first place
mortify	destroy, kill	**prevent**	precede, go before
murmur	complain	**principal**	most important
naught	useless	**principalities**	ranks, dignities
nay	no	**privily**	privately
nigh	near	**profane**	common, unholy
nought	nothing	**propitiation**	satisfaction
novice	new convert, beginner	**providence**	provision, foresight
nurture	development or training (includes discipline)	**provocation**	defiance
		prudence	practical understanding
oblation	sacrifice, offering	**publicans**	tax collectors
odious	offensive, disgusting	**purged**	cleansed
offscouring	filth, refuse cleaned off and thrown away	**purloining**	stealing
		quench	put out, extinguish
oft	often	**quicken**	make alive
ofttimes	often	**quit**	act
peculiar	special, particular	**railer**	one using bitter, abusive speech
penny	equal to about a day's labor	**raiment**	clothing
peradventure	perhaps	**reckon**	consider
perdition	destruction	**reckoned**	counted
peril	danger	**recompense**	reward
perseverance	patient effort	**record**	witness
pestilent	dangerous	**refuge**	safety
potsherd	piece of broken pottery	**regardeth**	considers
		regeneration	new birth
prating	speaking in a foolish, vain way	**remission**	forgiveness
		remnant	small remainder
pray	ask, beg	**rend**	tear, rip
predestinated	decreed beforehand	**render**	repay
		renown	great fame

rent	torn, pulled apart	sevenfold	seven times
repentance	change of mind	severally	separately
reproach	shame, blame	shamefacedness	great modesty, shyness
reprobate	rejected, condemned	shivers	fragments
reprobates	ones rejected	shunned	hesitated
revellings	noisy feasts, disorderly or immoral festival	signet	seal
		similitude	likeness
		simple (person)	easily misled, ignorant
reverence	respect, honor	slack	slow, idle
reviled	verbally abused	slain	killed
riddance	removal	slay	kill
rigour	severity	sleep	die
rioting	loose living	slew	killed
saints	ones set apart	slothful	lazy, inactive
salutation	greeting	sluggard	habitually lazy person
salute	greet		
sanctify	set apart	slumbereth	sleeps
scall	scaly or scabby skin	smite	strike
		smote	hit hard
scoffers	mockers	snares	traps
scorner	one who mocks at religion	sober	discreet, self-controlled
scornest	mock at	sobriety	self-control
scourge	whip		
scourgeth	whips	sojourn	stay, dwell, live temporarily
sect	religious group		
seducers	deceivers	sojourning	temporary stay
seed	descendants (when referring to people)	somewhat	a little
		sop	bread dipped in liquid
seemly	fitting, appropriate	sore	exceedingly
seethe	boil	sound	healthy
selfsame	the very same		
sepulchre	tomb, grave		

span	distance from extended little finger to thumb	**surety**	one responsible for another's debts
spoils	goods taken in battle	**surmisings**	guesses
spue	vomit	**swellings**	pride
stablish	establish	**swine**	pigs
staves	staffs, bars	**tabernacle**	temporary shelter
stead	place	**taches**	fasteners: clasps, buckles, hooks
steadfastly	constantly	**talebearer**	a gossip
stewards	managers	**tarry**	remain, stay, wait
straightly	urgently	**tattlers**	gossips
straightway	immediately	**temperance**	self-control
strait	narrow place, difficulty	**temporal**	temporary
strife	conflict, struggle	**tenons**	projections from wood to fit into a hole or socket
striker	a quarrelsome man	**terrible**	fear producing
stripes	blood trickling wounds	**testament**	will, covenant
strive	struggle, fight	**tetrarch**	ruler of part of Roman province
subjection	obedience	**thence**	there (place or time)
subtil	crafty, sly	**thenceforth**	from that time onward, after that
subtilty	craftiness	**therein**	in there
subvert	overturn, corrupt	**thereinto**	into it
subverted	corrupted	**thereof**	of it
succoured	helped, aided	**thereon**	on it
succourer	helper	**thereupon**	upon it
suffer	permit, allow; also means to experience hardship or pain	**therewith**	with it
		thither	there
sup	have supper	**thitherward**	toward that place
superfluity	overflowing	**threescore**	60 (a score equals 20)
superfluous	unnecessary		
supplication	humble request	**thrice**	three times

tidings	news	**veil**	curtain
tithes	tenth portions	**vengeance**	revenge
token	sign, symbol	**verily**	truly
tormented	tortured	**vesture**	garment, clothing
transgressor	lawbreaker	**vex**	to trouble or disturb
travail	intense pain		
travaileth	works very hard, toils	**vexation**	trouble, distress
		victuals	articles of food
tribulation	affliction	**vipers**	poisonous snakes
tribute	tax	**virtue**	power, goodness
tumult	uproar, loud commotion	**virtuous**	strong, chaste, morally good
twain	two	**vocation**	calling
unawares	without knowing	**void**	empty, useless
unction	anointing	**wanteth**	lacks
unfeigned	genuine, real, sincere	**wantonness**	unbridled lust
		ward	guardhouse, jail, prison
untoward	stubbornly willful, not easily controlled		
		watchings	wakefulness
		wax	grow, become
unwittingly	unknowingly	**waxed**	grew, became
upbraid	rebuke sharply	**waxen**	grown, become
upbraideth	rebukes severely	**wen**	lump on body
upright	straight, erect	**whatsoever**	whatever
usurp	unjustly take	**whence**	from where
usury	collecting high interest	**whensoever**	whenever
		whereas	although, while
utter	speak, tell	**whereby**	by which
uttermost	farthest	**wherefore**	for this cause, why
vain jangling	foolishness, meaningless talk		
		whereof	of which
vale	valley	**whereon**	on which
vanity	worthless, vain	**whereunto**	to what
variance	quarrel, strife	**wherewith**	with what
vehemently	strongly, intensely	**wherewithal**	with what

whether	if, which	**wiles**	sly tricks
whiles	while	**wist**	knew
whilst	while	**withal**	therewith, with that, with
whit	a bit (small amount)	**wont**	accustomed
whither	where	**wormwood**	poisonous root, bitterness
whithersoever	wherever		
whomsoever	whomever	**wot**	know
whoredom	prostitution, fornication	**wrest**	twist
		wroth	angry
whoremonger	one who is a fornicator	**wrought**	worked
		yea	yes
whoso	whoever		
whosoever	whoever		

Sources for Dictionary

Strong, James, *Strong's Concordance*. Power BibleCD program by Online Publishing, Inc. by Phil Linder, 2000.

Waite, D.A., *The Defined King James Bible*. Collingswood, New Jersey: The Bible for Today Press, 1999.

Webster, Noah, *Noah Webster's 1828 Dictionary of American English*. Franklin, TN: e-Sword by Rick Meyers, 2000-2008.

How to Get Started with Your Time with God

Getting started is the most important thing! The Bible gives us many examples of godly men who sought the Lord, as well as clear principles about how to do it. Here are some practical ideas to help you begin a walk with the Lord:

1. Find a quiet place to be with God.
   (Matthew 6:6, Daniel 6:10, Luke 6:12)

2. Try to be alone with God.
   (Luke 5:16, Mark 6:46, Matthew 14:23)

3. Choose a time in the morning to be with God.
   (Psalm 63:1, Proverbs 8:17, Psalm 5:3, Mark 1:35, Psalm 119:147, Genesis 19:27, Job 1:5)

4. Spend time with God every day.
   (Job 1:5, Daniel 6:10, Psalm 55:17, Psalm 145:2, Psalm 86:3, Psalm 88:9, Proverbs 8:34, Matthew 6:11, Acts 17:11, II Corinthians 4:16)

5. Do not hurry through your time with God.
   (Psalm 27:14, Psalm 46:10, Isaiah 40:31)

6. Have a desire to be with God.
   (Jeremiah 29:13, Psalm 16:11, Psalm 19:10, Psalm 63:1-2, Psalm 119:2, Psalm 119:16)

7. Go to bed early so that you can get up early and spend time with God. *(Psalm 127:2)*

8. Have a place to read in your Bible. There is no right or wrong way to read in your Bible. For those who are just starting out, I recommend that they read through the New Testament in a year. It requires reading only a chapter or less per day. Obviously, you can read other places, too! For instance, *Proverbs* provides practical wisdom, and *Psalms* lends great comfort.

Weekly Journal

SPECIAL PRAYER REQUESTS

This week's memory verse:

_____   _____

_____   _____

Sunday's Reading: **Date:**

God's Message to Me: _____

_____

_____

_____

_____

Monday's Reading: **Date:**

God's Message to Me: _____

_____

_____

_____

_____

Tuesday's Reading: **Date:**

God's Message to Me: _____

_____

_____

_____

_____

Wednesday's Reading: **Date:**

God's Message to Me: _____
_____
_____
_____
_____

Thursday's Reading: **Date:**

God's Message to Me: _____
_____
_____
_____
_____

Friday's Reading: **Date:**

God's Message to Me: _____
_____
_____
_____
_____

Saturday's Reading: **Date:**

God's Message to Me: _____
_____
_____
_____
_____

Weekly Journal

SPECIAL PRAYER REQUESTS

_____   _____

_____   _____

Sunday's Reading: Date:

God's Message to Me: _____

_____

_____

_____

_____

Monday's Reading: Date:

God's Message to Me: _____

_____

_____

_____

_____

Tuesday's Reading: Date:

God's Message to Me: _____

_____

_____

_____

_____

Wednesday's Reading: **Date:**

God's Message to Me: _____

_____

_____

_____

_____

Thursday's Reading: **Date:**

God's Message to Me: _____

_____

_____

_____

_____

Friday's Reading: **Date:**

God's Message to Me: _____

_____

_____

_____

_____

Saturday's Reading: **Date:**

God's Message to Me: _____

_____

_____

_____

_____

Weekly Journal

SPECIAL PRAYER REQUESTS

This week's memory verse:

_____ _____

_____ _____

Sunday's Reading: **Date:**

God's Message to Me: _____

_____

_____

_____

_____

Monday's Reading: **Date:**

God's Message to Me: _____

_____

_____

_____

_____

Tuesday's Reading: **Date:**

God's Message to Me: _____

_____

_____

_____

_____

Wednesday's Reading: **Date:**

God's Message to Me: _____

_____

_____

_____

_____

Thursday's Reading: **Date:**

God's Message to Me: _____

_____

_____

_____

_____

Friday's Reading: **Date:**

God's Message to Me: _____

_____

_____

_____

_____

Saturday's Reading: **Date:**

God's Message to Me: _____

_____

_____

_____

_____

Weekly Journal

SPECIAL PRAYER REQUESTS

This week's memory verse:

_____ _____

_____ _____

Sunday's Reading: **Date:**

God's Message to Me: _____

_____

_____

_____

_____

Monday's Reading: **Date:**

God's Message to Me: _____

_____

_____

_____

_____

Tuesday's Reading: **Date:**

God's Message to Me: _____

_____

_____

_____

_____

Wednesday's Reading: **Date:**

God's Message to Me: _____

_____

_____

_____

_____

Thursday's Reading: **Date:**

God's Message to Me: _____

_____

_____

_____

_____

Friday's Reading: **Date:**

God's Message to Me: _____

_____

_____

_____

_____

Saturday's Reading: **Date:**

God's Message to Me: _____

_____

_____

_____

_____

Weekly Journal

SPECIAL PRAYER REQUESTS

This week's memory verse:

_____   _____

_____   _____

Sunday's Reading: Date: _____

God's Message to Me: _____

_____

_____

_____

_____

Monday's Reading: Date: _____

God's Message to Me: _____

_____

_____

_____

_____

Tuesday's Reading: Date: _____

God's Message to Me: _____

_____

_____

_____

_____

Wednesday's Reading: **Date:**

God's Message to Me: _____

_____

_____

_____

_____

Thursday's Reading: **Date:**

God's Message to Me: _____

_____

_____

_____

_____

Friday's Reading: **Date:**

God's Message to Me: _____

_____

_____

_____

_____

Saturday's Reading: **Date:**

God's Message to Me: _____

_____

_____

_____

_____

Weekly Journal

SPECIAL PRAYER REQUESTS

This week's memory verse:

_____ _____

_____ _____

Sunday's Reading: **Date:**

God's Message to Me: _____

_____

_____

_____

_____

Monday's Reading: **Date:**

God's Message to Me: _____

_____

_____

_____

_____

Tuesday's Reading: **Date:**

God's Message to Me: _____

_____

_____

_____

_____

Wednesday's Reading: **Date:**

God's Message to Me: _____

_____

_____

_____

_____

Thursday's Reading: **Date:**

God's Message to Me: _____

_____

_____

_____

_____

Friday's Reading: **Date:**

God's Message to Me: _____

_____

_____

_____

_____

Saturday's Reading: **Date:**

God's Message to Me: _____

_____

_____

_____

_____

Weekly Journal

SPECIAL PRAYER REQUESTS

This week's memory verse:

_____ _____

_____ _____

Sunday's Reading: **Date:**

God's Message to Me: _____

_____

_____

_____

_____

Monday's Reading: **Date:**

God's Message to Me: _____

_____

_____

_____

_____

Tuesday's Reading: **Date:**

God's Message to Me: _____

_____

_____

_____

_____

Wednesday's Reading:　　　　　**Date:**

God's Message to Me: _____

_____

_____

_____

_____

Thursday's Reading:　　　　　**Date:**

God's Message to Me: _____

_____

_____

_____

_____

Friday's Reading:　　　　　**Date:**

God's Message to Me: _____

_____

_____

_____

_____

Saturday's Reading:　　　　　**Date:**

God's Message to Me: _____

_____

_____

_____

_____

 # Weekly Journal

SPECIAL PRAYER REQUESTS

This week's memory verse:

_____ _____

_____ _____

Sunday's Reading: **Date:**

God's Message to Me: _____

_____

_____

_____

_____

Monday's Reading: **Date:**

God's Message to Me: _____

_____

_____

_____

_____

Tuesday's Reading: **Date:**

God's Message to Me: _____

_____

_____

_____

_____

Wednesday's Reading: Date:

God's Message to Me: _____

_____

_____

_____

_____

Thursday's Reading: Date:

God's Message to Me: _____

_____

_____

_____

_____

Friday's Reading: Date:

God's Message to Me: _____

_____

_____

_____

_____

Saturday's Reading: Date:

God's Message to Me: _____

_____

_____

_____

_____

Weekly Journal

SPECIAL PRAYER REQUESTS

This week's memory verse:

_____ _____

_____ _____

Sunday's Reading: **Date:**

God's Message to Me: _____

_____

_____

_____

_____

Monday's Reading: **Date:**

God's Message to Me: _____

_____

_____

_____

_____

Tuesday's Reading: **Date:**

God's Message to Me: _____

_____

_____

_____

_____

Wednesday's Reading: **Date:**

God's Message to Me: _____

_____

_____

_____

_____

Thursday's Reading: **Date:**

God's Message to Me: _____

_____

_____

_____

_____

Friday's Reading: **Date:**

God's Message to Me: _____

_____

_____

_____

_____

Saturday's Reading: **Date:**

God's Message to Me: _____

_____

_____

_____

_____

Weekly Journal

SPECIAL PRAYER REQUESTS

This week's memory verse:

_____   _____

_____   _____

Sunday's Reading: **Date:**

God's Message to Me: _____

_____

_____

_____

_____

Monday's Reading: **Date:**

God's Message to Me: _____

_____

_____

_____

_____

Tuesday's Reading: **Date:**

God's Message to Me: _____

_____

_____

_____

_____

Wednesday's Reading: **Date:**

God's Message to Me: _____

_____

_____

_____

_____

Thursday's Reading: **Date:**

God's Message to Me: _____

_____

_____

_____

_____

Friday's Reading: **Date:**

God's Message to Me: _____

_____

_____

_____

_____

Saturday's Reading: **Date:**

God's Message to Me: _____

_____

_____

_____

_____

Weekly Journal

SPECIAL PRAYER REQUESTS

This week's memory verse:

_____ _____

_____ _____

Sunday's Reading: **Date:**

God's Message to Me: _____

_____

_____

_____

_____

Monday's Reading: **Date:**

God's Message to Me: _____

_____

_____

_____

_____

Tuesday's Reading: **Date:**

God's Message to Me: _____

_____

_____

_____

_____

Wednesday's Reading: **Date:**

God's Message to Me: _____

_____

_____

_____

_____

Thursday's Reading: **Date:**

God's Message to Me: _____

_____

_____

_____

_____

Friday's Reading: **Date:**

God's Message to Me: _____

_____

_____

_____

_____

Saturday's Reading: **Date:**

God's Message to Me: _____

_____

_____

_____

_____

Weekly Journal

SPECIAL PRAYER REQUESTS

This week's memory verse:

_____   _____

_____   _____

Sunday's Reading: **Date:**

God's Message to Me: _____

_____

_____

_____

_____

Monday's Reading: **Date:**

God's Message to Me: _____

_____

_____

_____

_____

Tuesday's Reading: **Date:**

God's Message to Me: _____

_____

_____

_____

_____

Wednesday's Reading: **Date:**

God's Message to Me: _____

_____

_____

_____

_____

Thursday's Reading: **Date:**

God's Message to Me: _____

_____

_____

_____

_____

Friday's Reading: **Date:**

God's Message to Me: _____

_____

_____

_____

_____

Saturday's Reading: **Date:**

God's Message to Me: _____

_____

_____

_____

_____

Weekly Journal

SPECIAL PRAYER REQUESTS

This week's memory verse:

_____   _____

_____   _____

Sunday's Reading: **Date:**

God's Message to Me: _____

_____

_____

_____

_____

Monday's Reading: **Date:**

God's Message to Me: _____

_____

_____

_____

_____

Tuesday's Reading: **Date:**

God's Message to Me: _____

_____

_____

_____

_____

Wednesday's Reading: Date:

God's Message to Me: _____
_____
_____
_____
_____

Thursday's Reading: Date:

God's Message to Me: _____
_____
_____
_____
_____

Friday's Reading: Date:

God's Message to Me: _____
_____
_____
_____
_____

Saturday's Reading: Date:

God's Message to Me: _____
_____
_____
_____
_____

Weekly Journal

SPECIAL PRAYER REQUESTS

This week's
memory verse:

_____   _____

_____   _____

Sunday's Reading: **Date:**

God's Message to Me: _____

_____

_____

_____

_____

Monday's Reading: **Date:**

God's Message to Me: _____

_____

_____

_____

_____

Tuesday's Reading: **Date:**

God's Message to Me: _____

_____

_____

_____

_____

Wednesday's Reading: **Date:**

God's Message to Me: _____

_____

_____

_____

_____

Thursday's Reading: **Date:**

God's Message to Me: _____

_____

_____

_____

_____

Friday's Reading: **Date:**

God's Message to Me: _____

_____

_____

_____

_____

Saturday's Reading: **Date:**

God's Message to Me: _____

_____

_____

_____

_____

Weekly Journal

SPECIAL PRAYER REQUESTS

This week's memory verse:

_____   _____

_____   _____

Sunday's Reading: **Date:**

God's Message to Me: _____

_____

_____

_____

_____

Monday's Reading: **Date:**

God's Message to Me: _____

_____

_____

_____

_____

Tuesday's Reading: **Date:**

God's Message to Me: _____

_____

_____

_____

_____

Wednesday's Reading: **Date:**

God's Message to Me: _____

_____

_____

_____

_____

Thursday's Reading: **Date:**

God's Message to Me: _____

_____

_____

_____

_____

Friday's Reading: **Date:**

God's Message to Me: _____

_____

_____

_____

_____

Saturday's Reading: **Date:**

God's Message to Me: _____

_____

_____

_____

_____

Weekly Journal

SPECIAL PRAYER REQUESTS

_____   _____

_____   _____

This week's memory verse:

Sunday's Reading: **Date:**

God's Message to Me: _____

_____

_____

_____

_____

Monday's Reading: **Date:**

God's Message to Me: _____

_____

_____

_____

_____

Tuesday's Reading: **Date:**

God's Message to Me: _____

_____

_____

_____

_____

Wednesday's Reading: **Date:**

God's Message to Me: _____

_____

_____

_____

_____

Thursday's Reading: **Date:**

God's Message to Me: _____

_____

_____

_____

_____

Friday's Reading: **Date:**

God's Message to Me: _____

_____

_____

_____

_____

Saturday's Reading: **Date:**

God's Message to Me: _____

_____

_____

_____

_____

Weekly Journal

SPECIAL PRAYER REQUESTS

This week's memory verse:

_____   _____

_____   _____

Sunday's Reading: **Date:**

God's Message to Me: _____

_____

_____

_____

_____

Monday's Reading: **Date:**

God's Message to Me: _____

_____

_____

_____

_____

Tuesday's Reading: **Date:**

God's Message to Me: _____

_____

_____

_____

_____

Wednesday's Reading: **Date:**

God's Message to Me: _____

_____

_____

_____

_____

Thursday's Reading: **Date:**

God's Message to Me: _____

_____

_____

_____

_____

Friday's Reading: **Date:**

God's Message to Me: _____

_____

_____

_____

_____

Saturday's Reading: **Date:**

God's Message to Me: _____

_____

_____

_____

_____

Weekly Journal

SPECIAL PRAYER REQUESTS

This week's memory verse:

_____   _____

_____   _____

Sunday's Reading: **Date:**

God's Message to Me: _____

_____

_____

_____

_____

Monday's Reading: **Date:**

God's Message to Me: _____

_____

_____

_____

_____

Tuesday's Reading: **Date:**

God's Message to Me: _____

_____

_____

_____

_____

Wednesday's Reading: **Date:**

God's Message to Me: _____

_____

_____

_____

_____

Thursday's Reading: **Date:**

God's Message to Me: _____

_____

_____

_____

_____

Friday's Reading: **Date:**

God's Message to Me: _____

_____

_____

_____

_____

Saturday's Reading: **Date:**

God's Message to Me: _____

_____

_____

_____

_____

Weekly Journal

SPECIAL PRAYER REQUESTS

_____   _____

_____   _____

This week's memory verse:

Sunday's Reading: **Date:**

God's Message to Me: _____

_____

_____

_____

_____

Monday's Reading: **Date:**

God's Message to Me: _____

_____

_____

_____

_____

Tuesday's Reading: **Date:**

God's Message to Me: _____

_____

_____

_____

_____

Wednesday's Reading: **Date:**

God's Message to Me: _____

_____

_____

_____

_____

Thursday's Reading: **Date:**

God's Message to Me: _____

_____

_____

_____

_____

Friday's Reading: **Date:**

God's Message to Me: _____

_____

_____

_____

_____

Saturday's Reading: **Date:**

God's Message to Me: _____

_____

_____

_____

_____

Weekly Journal

SPECIAL PRAYER REQUESTS

This week's memory verse:

_____ _____

_____ _____

Sunday's Reading: **Date:**

God's Message to Me: _____

_____

_____

_____

_____

Monday's Reading: **Date:**

God's Message to Me: _____

_____

_____

_____

_____

Tuesday's Reading: **Date:**

God's Message to Me: _____

_____

_____

_____

_____

Wednesday's Reading: **Date:**

God's Message to Me: _____

_____

_____

_____

_____

Thursday's Reading: **Date:**

God's Message to Me: _____

_____

_____

_____

_____

Friday's Reading: **Date:**

God's Message to Me: _____

_____

_____

_____

_____

Saturday's Reading: **Date:**

God's Message to Me: _____

_____

_____

_____

_____

Weekly Journal

SPECIAL PRAYER REQUESTS

This week's memory verse:

_____ _____

_____ _____

Sunday's Reading:　　　　　　　　**Date:**

God's Message to Me: _____

_____

_____

_____

_____

Monday's Reading:　　　　　　　　**Date:**

God's Message to Me: _____

_____

_____

_____

_____

Tuesday's Reading:　　　　　　　　**Date:**

God's Message to Me: _____

_____

_____

_____

_____

Wednesday's Reading: **Date:**

God's Message to Me: _____

_____

_____

_____

_____

Thursday's Reading: **Date:**

God's Message to Me: _____

_____

_____

_____

_____

Friday's Reading: **Date:**

God's Message to Me: _____

_____

_____

_____

_____

Saturday's Reading: **Date:**

God's Message to Me: _____

_____

_____

_____

_____

Weekly Journal

SPECIAL PRAYER REQUESTS

This week's memory verse:

_____   _____

_____   _____

Sunday's Reading: **Date:**

God's Message to Me: _____

_____

_____

_____

_____

Monday's Reading: **Date:**

God's Message to Me: _____

_____

_____

_____

_____

Tuesday's Reading: **Date:**

God's Message to Me: _____

_____

_____

_____

_____

Wednesday's Reading: **Date:**

God's Message to Me: _____

_____

_____

_____

_____

Thursday's Reading: **Date:**

God's Message to Me: _____

_____

_____

_____

_____

Friday's Reading: **Date:**

God's Message to Me: _____

_____

_____

_____

_____

Saturday's Reading: **Date:**

God's Message to Me: _____

_____

_____

_____

_____

Weekly Journal

SPECIAL PRAYER REQUESTS

_____   _____

_____   _____

This week's memory verse:

Sunday's Reading: **Date:**

God's Message to Me: _____

_____

_____

_____

_____

Monday's Reading: **Date:**

God's Message to Me: _____

_____

_____

_____

_____

Tuesday's Reading: **Date:**

God's Message to Me: _____

_____

_____

_____

_____

Wednesday's Reading: **Date:**

God's Message to Me: _____
_____
_____
_____
_____

Thursday's Reading: **Date:**

God's Message to Me: _____
_____
_____
_____
_____

Friday's Reading: **Date:**

God's Message to Me: _____
_____
_____
_____
_____

Saturday's Reading: **Date:**

God's Message to Me: _____
_____
_____
_____
_____

Weekly Journal

SPECIAL PRAYER REQUESTS

This week's memory verse:

_____ _____

_____ _____

Sunday's Reading: **Date:**

God's Message to Me: _____

_____

_____

_____

_____

Monday's Reading: **Date:**

God's Message to Me: _____

_____

_____

_____

_____

Tuesday's Reading: **Date:**

God's Message to Me: _____

_____

_____

_____

_____

Wednesday's Reading: **Date:**

God's Message to Me: _____

_____

_____

_____

_____

Thursday's Reading: **Date:**

God's Message to Me: _____

_____

_____

_____

_____

Friday's Reading: **Date:**

God's Message to Me: _____

_____

_____

_____

_____

Saturday's Reading: **Date:**

God's Message to Me: _____

_____

_____

_____

_____

Weekly Journal

SPECIAL PRAYER REQUESTS

This week's memory verse:

_____   _____

_____   _____

Sunday's Reading: **Date:**

God's Message to Me: _____

_____

_____

_____

_____

Monday's Reading: **Date:**

God's Message to Me: _____

_____

_____

_____

_____

Tuesday's Reading: **Date:**

God's Message to Me: _____

_____

_____

_____

_____

Wednesday's Reading: **Date:**

God's Message to Me: _____

_____

_____

_____

_____

Thursday's Reading: **Date:**

God's Message to Me: _____

_____

_____

_____

_____

Friday's Reading: **Date:**

God's Message to Me: _____

_____

_____

_____

_____

Saturday's Reading: **Date:**

God's Message to Me: _____

_____

_____

_____

_____

Weekly Journal

SPECIAL PRAYER REQUESTS

This week's memory verse:

_____ _____

_____ _____

Sunday's Reading: **Date:**

God's Message to Me: _____

_____

_____

_____

_____

Monday's Reading: **Date:**

God's Message to Me: _____

_____

_____

_____

_____

Tuesday's Reading: **Date:**

God's Message to Me: _____

_____

_____

_____

_____

Wednesday's Reading: **Date:**

God's Message to Me: _____

_____

_____

_____

_____

Thursday's Reading: **Date:**

God's Message to Me: _____

_____

_____

_____

_____

Friday's Reading: **Date:**

God's Message to Me: _____

_____

_____

_____

_____

Saturday's Reading: **Date:**

God's Message to Me: _____

_____

_____

_____

_____

Weekly Journal

SPECIAL PRAYER REQUESTS

This week's memory verse:

_____ _____

_____ _____

Sunday's Reading: **Date:**

God's Message to Me: _____

_____

_____

_____

_____

Monday's Reading: **Date:**

God's Message to Me: _____

_____

_____

_____

_____

Tuesday's Reading: **Date:**

God's Message to Me: _____

_____

_____

_____

_____

Wednesday's Reading: **Date:**

God's Message to Me: _____

_____

_____

_____

_____

Thursday's Reading: **Date:**

God's Message to Me: _____

_____

_____

_____

_____

Friday's Reading: **Date:**

God's Message to Me: _____

_____

_____

_____

_____

Saturday's Reading: **Date:**

God's Message to Me: _____

_____

_____

_____

_____

Weekly Journal

SPECIAL PRAYER REQUESTS

This week's memory verse:

_____   _____

_____   _____

Sunday's Reading: **Date:**

God's Message to Me: _____

_____

_____

_____

_____

Monday's Reading: **Date:**

God's Message to Me: _____

_____

_____

_____

_____

Tuesday's Reading: **Date:**

God's Message to Me: _____

_____

_____

_____

_____

Wednesday's Reading: **Date:**

God's Message to Me: _____

_____

_____

_____

_____

Thursday's Reading: **Date:**

God's Message to Me: _____

_____

_____

_____

_____

Friday's Reading: **Date:**

God's Message to Me: _____

_____

_____

_____

_____

Saturday's Reading: **Date:**

God's Message to Me: _____

_____

_____

_____

_____

Weekly Journal

SPECIAL PRAYER REQUESTS

_____ _____

_____ _____

This week's memory verse:

Sunday's Reading: **Date:**

God's Message to Me: _____

_____

_____

_____

_____

Monday's Reading: **Date:**

God's Message to Me: _____

_____

_____

_____

_____

Tuesday's Reading: **Date:**

God's Message to Me: _____

_____

_____

_____

_____

Wednesday's Reading: **Date:**

God's Message to Me: _____

_____

_____

_____

_____

Thursday's Reading: **Date:**

God's Message to Me: _____

_____

_____

_____

_____

Friday's Reading: **Date:**

God's Message to Me: _____

_____

_____

_____

_____

Saturday's Reading: **Date:**

God's Message to Me: _____

_____

_____

_____

_____

Weekly Journal

SPECIAL PRAYER REQUESTS

This week's memory verse:

_____   _____

_____   _____

Sunday's Reading: **Date:**

God's Message to Me: _____

_____

_____

_____

_____

Monday's Reading: **Date:**

God's Message to Me: _____

_____

_____

_____

_____

Tuesday's Reading: **Date:**

God's Message to Me: _____

_____

_____

_____

_____

Wednesday's Reading: **Date:**

God's Message to Me: _____

_____

_____

_____

_____

Thursday's Reading: **Date:**

God's Message to Me: _____

_____

_____

_____

_____

Friday's Reading: **Date:**

God's Message to Me: _____

_____

_____

_____

_____

Saturday's Reading: **Date:**

God's Message to Me: _____

_____

_____

_____

_____

 **Weekly Journal**

SPECIAL PRAYER REQUESTS

This week's memory verse:

_____ _____

_____ _____

Sunday's Reading: **Date:**

God's Message to Me: _____

_____

_____

_____

_____

Monday's Reading: **Date:**

God's Message to Me: _____

_____

_____

_____

_____

Tuesday's Reading: **Date:**

God's Message to Me: _____

_____

_____

_____

_____

Wednesday's Reading: **Date:**

God's Message to Me: _____

_____

_____

_____

_____

Thursday's Reading: **Date:**

God's Message to Me: _____

_____

_____

_____

_____

Friday's Reading: **Date:**

God's Message to Me: _____

_____

_____

_____

_____

Saturday's Reading: **Date:**

God's Message to Me: _____

_____

_____

_____

_____

Weekly Journal

SPECIAL PRAYER REQUESTS

_____   _____

_____   _____

Sunday's Reading: **Date:**

God's Message to Me: _____

_____

_____

_____

_____

Monday's Reading: **Date:**

God's Message to Me: _____

_____

_____

_____

_____

Tuesday's Reading: **Date:**

God's Message to Me: _____

_____

_____

_____

_____

Wednesday's Reading: **Date:**

God's Message to Me: _____

_____

_____

_____

_____

Thursday's Reading: **Date:**

God's Message to Me: _____

_____

_____

_____

_____

Friday's Reading: **Date:**

God's Message to Me: _____

_____

_____

_____

_____

Saturday's Reading: **Date:**

God's Message to Me: _____

_____

_____

_____

_____

Weekly Journal

SPECIAL PRAYER REQUESTS

This week's memory verse:

_____   _____

_____   _____

Sunday's Reading: **Date:**

God's Message to Me: _____

_____

_____

_____

_____

Monday's Reading: **Date:**

God's Message to Me: _____

_____

_____

_____

_____

Tuesday's Reading: **Date:**

God's Message to Me: _____

_____

_____

_____

_____

Wednesday's Reading: **Date:**

God's Message to Me: _____
_____
_____
_____
_____

Thursday's Reading: **Date:**

God's Message to Me: _____
_____
_____
_____
_____

Friday's Reading: **Date:**

God's Message to Me: _____
_____
_____
_____
_____

Saturday's Reading: **Date:**

God's Message to Me: _____
_____
_____
_____
_____

 # Weekly Journal

SPECIAL PRAYER REQUESTS

This week's memory verse:

_____   _____

_____   _____

Sunday's Reading: **Date:**

God's Message to Me: _____

_____

_____

_____

_____

Monday's Reading: **Date:**

God's Message to Me: _____

_____

_____

_____

_____

Tuesday's Reading: **Date:**

God's Message to Me: _____

_____

_____

_____

_____

Wednesday's Reading:　　　　　**Date:**

God's Message to Me: _____

_____

_____

_____

_____

Thursday's Reading:　　　　　**Date:**

God's Message to Me: _____

_____

_____

_____

_____

Friday's Reading:　　　　　**Date:**

God's Message to Me: _____

_____

_____

_____

_____

Saturday's Reading:　　　　　**Date:**

God's Message to Me: _____

_____

_____

_____

_____

Weekly Journal

SPECIAL PRAYER REQUESTS

This week's memory verse:

_____   _____

_____   _____

Sunday's Reading: **Date:**

God's Message to Me: _____

_____

_____

_____

_____

Monday's Reading: **Date:**

God's Message to Me: _____

_____

_____

_____

_____

Tuesday's Reading: **Date:**

God's Message to Me: _____

_____

_____

_____

_____

Wednesday's Reading:　　　　　**Date:**

God's Message to Me: _____

_____

_____

_____

_____

Thursday's Reading:　　　　　**Date:**

God's Message to Me: _____

_____

_____

_____

_____

Friday's Reading:　　　　　**Date:**

God's Message to Me: _____

_____

_____

_____

_____

Saturday's Reading:　　　　　**Date:**

God's Message to Me: _____

_____

_____

_____

_____

Weekly Journal

SPECIAL PRAYER REQUESTS

_____   _____

_____   _____

Sunday's Reading: **Date:**

God's Message to Me: _____

_____

_____

_____

_____

Monday's Reading: **Date:**

God's Message to Me: _____

_____

_____

_____

_____

Tuesday's Reading: **Date:**

God's Message to Me: _____

_____

_____

_____

_____

Wednesday's Reading: **Date:**

God's Message to Me: _____

_____

_____

_____

_____

Thursday's Reading: **Date:**

God's Message to Me: _____

_____

_____

_____

_____

Friday's Reading: **Date:**

God's Message to Me: _____

_____

_____

_____

_____

Saturday's Reading: **Date:**

God's Message to Me: _____

_____

_____

_____

_____

Weekly Journal

SPECIAL PRAYER REQUESTS

This week's memory verse:

_____   _____

_____   _____

Sunday's Reading: **Date:**

God's Message to Me: _____

_____

_____

_____

_____

Monday's Reading: **Date:**

God's Message to Me: _____

_____

_____

_____

_____

Tuesday's Reading: **Date:**

God's Message to Me: _____

_____

_____

_____

_____

Wednesday's Reading: **Date:**

God's Message to Me: _____

_____

_____

_____

_____

Thursday's Reading: **Date:**

God's Message to Me: _____

_____

_____

_____

_____

Friday's Reading: **Date:**

God's Message to Me: _____

_____

_____

_____

_____

Saturday's Reading: **Date:**

God's Message to Me: _____

_____

_____

_____

_____

Weekly Journal

SPECIAL PRAYER REQUESTS

This week's memory verse:

_____   _____

_____   _____

Sunday's Reading: **Date:**

God's Message to Me: _____

_____

_____

_____

_____

Monday's Reading: **Date:**

God's Message to Me: _____

_____

_____

_____

_____

Tuesday's Reading: **Date:**

God's Message to Me: _____

_____

_____

_____

_____

Wednesday's Reading: **Date:**

God's Message to Me: _____
_____
_____
_____
_____

Thursday's Reading: **Date:**

God's Message to Me: _____
_____
_____
_____
_____

Friday's Reading: **Date:**

God's Message to Me: _____
_____
_____
_____
_____

Saturday's Reading: **Date:**

God's Message to Me: _____
_____
_____
_____
_____

Weekly Journal

SPECIAL PRAYER REQUESTS

This week's memory verse:

_____ _____

_____ _____

Sunday's Reading: Date:

God's Message to Me: _____

_____

_____

_____

_____

Monday's Reading: Date:

God's Message to Me: _____

_____

_____

_____

_____

Tuesday's Reading: Date:

God's Message to Me: _____

_____

_____

_____

_____

Wednesday's Reading: **Date:**

God's Message to Me: _____

_____

_____

_____

_____

Thursday's Reading: **Date:**

God's Message to Me: _____

_____

_____

_____

_____

Friday's Reading: **Date:**

God's Message to Me: _____

_____

_____

_____

_____

Saturday's Reading: **Date:**

God's Message to Me: _____

_____

_____

_____

_____

# Weekly Journal

SPECIAL PRAYER REQUESTS

This week's memory verse:

_____ _____

_____ _____

Sunday's Reading: **Date:**

God's Message to Me: _____

_____

_____

_____

_____

Monday's Reading: **Date:**

God's Message to Me: _____

_____

_____

_____

_____

Tuesday's Reading: **Date:**

God's Message to Me: _____

_____

_____

_____

_____

Wednesday's Reading: **Date:**

God's Message to Me: _____

_____

_____

_____

_____

Thursday's Reading: **Date:**

God's Message to Me: _____

_____

_____

_____

_____

Friday's Reading: **Date:**

God's Message to Me: _____

_____

_____

_____

_____

Saturday's Reading: **Date:**

God's Message to Me: _____

_____

_____

_____

_____

Weekly Journal

SPECIAL PRAYER REQUESTS

This week's memory verse:

_____   _____

_____   _____

Sunday's Reading: **Date:**

God's Message to Me: _____

_____

_____

_____

_____

Monday's Reading: **Date:**

God's Message to Me: _____

_____

_____

_____

_____

Tuesday's Reading: **Date:**

God's Message to Me: _____

_____

_____

_____

_____

Wednesday's Reading: **Date:**

God's Message to Me: _____

_____

_____

_____

_____

Thursday's Reading: **Date:**

God's Message to Me: _____

_____

_____

_____

_____

Friday's Reading: **Date:**

God's Message to Me: _____

_____

_____

_____

_____

Saturday's Reading: **Date:**

God's Message to Me: _____

_____

_____

_____

_____

Weekly Journal

SPECIAL PRAYER REQUESTS

This week's memory verse:

_____   _____

_____   _____

Sunday's Reading: **Date:**

God's Message to Me: _____

_____

_____

_____

_____

Monday's Reading: **Date:**

God's Message to Me: _____

_____

_____

_____

_____

Tuesday's Reading: **Date:**

God's Message to Me: _____

_____

_____

_____

_____

Wednesday's Reading: **Date:**

God's Message to Me: _____

_____

_____

_____

_____

Thursday's Reading: **Date:**

God's Message to Me: _____

_____

_____

_____

_____

Friday's Reading: **Date:**

God's Message to Me: _____

_____

_____

_____

_____

Saturday's Reading: **Date:**

God's Message to Me: _____

_____

_____

_____

_____

Weekly Journal

SPECIAL PRAYER REQUESTS

This week's memory verse:

_____   _____

_____   _____

Sunday's Reading: **Date:**

God's Message to Me: _____

_____

_____

_____

_____

Monday's Reading: **Date:**

God's Message to Me: _____

_____

_____

_____

_____

Tuesday's Reading: **Date:**

God's Message to Me: _____

_____

_____

_____

_____

Wednesday's Reading: **Date:**

God's Message to Me: _____
_____
_____
_____
_____

Thursday's Reading: **Date:**

God's Message to Me: _____
_____
_____
_____
_____

Friday's Reading: **Date:**

God's Message to Me: _____
_____
_____
_____
_____

Saturday's Reading: **Date:**

God's Message to Me: _____
_____
_____
_____
_____

Weekly Journal

SPECIAL PRAYER REQUESTS

This week's memory verse:

_____ _____

_____ _____

Sunday's Reading: Date:

God's Message to Me: _____

_____

_____

_____

_____

Monday's Reading: Date:

God's Message to Me: _____

_____

_____

_____

_____

Tuesday's Reading: Date:

God's Message to Me: _____

_____

_____

_____

_____

Wednesday's Reading: **Date:**

God's Message to Me: _____

_____

_____

_____

_____

Thursday's Reading: **Date:**

God's Message to Me: _____

_____

_____

_____

_____

Friday's Reading: **Date:**

God's Message to Me: _____

_____

_____

_____

_____

Saturday's Reading: **Date:**

God's Message to Me: _____

_____

_____

_____

_____

Weekly Journal

SPECIAL PRAYER REQUESTS

_____ _____

_____ _____

Sunday's Reading: **Date:**

God's Message to Me: _____

_____

_____

_____

_____

Monday's Reading: **Date:**

God's Message to Me: _____

_____

_____

_____

_____

Tuesday's Reading: **Date:**

God's Message to Me: _____

_____

_____

_____

_____

Wednesday's Reading: **Date:**

God's Message to Me: _____

_____

_____

_____

_____

Thursday's Reading: **Date:**

God's Message to Me: _____

_____

_____

_____

_____

Friday's Reading: **Date:**

God's Message to Me: _____

_____

_____

_____

_____

Saturday's Reading: **Date:**

God's Message to Me: _____

_____

_____

_____

_____

Weekly Journal

SPECIAL PRAYER REQUESTS

This week's memory verse:

_____   _____

_____   _____

Sunday's Reading: **Date:**

God's Message to Me: _____

_____

_____

_____

_____

Monday's Reading: **Date:**

God's Message to Me: _____

_____

_____

_____

_____

Tuesday's Reading: **Date:**

God's Message to Me: _____

_____

_____

_____

_____

Wednesday's Reading: **Date:**

God's Message to Me: _____

_____

_____

_____

_____

Thursday's Reading: **Date:**

God's Message to Me: _____

_____

_____

_____

_____

Friday's Reading: **Date:**

God's Message to Me: _____

_____

_____

_____

_____

Saturday's Reading: **Date:**

God's Message to Me: _____

_____

_____

_____

_____

Weekly Journal

SPECIAL PRAYER REQUESTS

This week's memory verse:

_____   _____

_____   _____

Sunday's Reading: **Date:**

God's Message to Me: _____

_____

_____

_____

_____

Monday's Reading: **Date:**

God's Message to Me: _____

_____

_____

_____

_____

Tuesday's Reading: **Date:**

God's Message to Me: _____

_____

_____

_____

_____

Wednesday's Reading: **Date:**

God's Message to Me: _____

_____

_____

_____

_____

Thursday's Reading: **Date:**

God's Message to Me: _____

_____

_____

_____

_____

Friday's Reading: **Date:**

God's Message to Me: _____

_____

_____

_____

_____

Saturday's Reading: **Date:**

God's Message to Me: _____

_____

_____

_____

_____

Weekly Journal

SPECIAL PRAYER REQUESTS

This week's memory verse:

_____   _____

_____   _____

Sunday's Reading: **Date:**

God's Message to Me: _____

_____

_____

_____

_____

Monday's Reading: **Date:**

God's Message to Me: _____

_____

_____

_____

_____

Tuesday's Reading: **Date:**

God's Message to Me: _____

_____

_____

_____

_____

Wednesday's Reading: **Date:**

God's Message to Me: _____
_____
_____
_____
_____

Thursday's Reading: **Date:**

God's Message to Me: _____
_____
_____
_____
_____

Friday's Reading: **Date:**

God's Message to Me: _____
_____
_____
_____
_____

Saturday's Reading: **Date:**

God's Message to Me: _____
_____
_____
_____
_____

Weekly Journal

SPECIAL PRAYER REQUESTS

_____   _____

_____   _____

This week's memory verse:

Sunday's Reading: Date:

God's Message to Me: _____

_____

_____

_____

_____

Monday's Reading: Date:

God's Message to Me: _____

_____

_____

_____

_____

Tuesday's Reading: Date:

God's Message to Me: _____

_____

_____

_____

_____

Wednesday's Reading: **Date:**

God's Message to Me: _____

_____

_____

_____

_____

Thursday's Reading: **Date:**

God's Message to Me: _____

_____

_____

_____

_____

Friday's Reading: **Date:**

God's Message to Me: _____

_____

_____

_____

_____

Saturday's Reading: **Date:**

God's Message to Me: _____

_____

_____

_____

_____

Weekly Journal

SPECIAL PRAYER REQUESTS

This week's memory verse:

_____   _____

_____   _____

Sunday's Reading: Date:

God's Message to Me: _____

_____

_____

_____

_____

Monday's Reading: Date:

God's Message to Me: _____

_____

_____

_____

_____

Tuesday's Reading: Date:

God's Message to Me: _____

_____

_____

_____

_____

Wednesday's Reading: **Date:**

God's Message to Me: _____

_____

_____

_____

_____

Thursday's Reading: **Date:**

God's Message to Me: _____

_____

_____

_____

_____

Friday's Reading: **Date:**

God's Message to Me: _____

_____

_____

_____

_____

Saturday's Reading: **Date:**

God's Message to Me: _____

_____

_____

_____

_____

Weekly Journal

SPECIAL PRAYER REQUESTS

This week's memory verse:

_____ _____

_____ _____

Sunday's Reading: **Date:**

God's Message to Me: _____

_____

_____

_____

_____

Monday's Reading: **Date:**

God's Message to Me: _____

_____

_____

_____

_____

Tuesday's Reading: **Date:**

God's Message to Me: _____

_____

_____

_____

_____

Wednesday's Reading: **Date:**

God's Message to Me: _____

_____

_____

_____

_____

Thursday's Reading: **Date:**

God's Message to Me: _____

_____

_____

_____

_____

Friday's Reading: **Date:**

God's Message to Me: _____

_____

_____

_____

_____

Saturday's Reading: **Date:**

God's Message to Me: _____

_____

_____

_____

_____

Weekly Journal

SPECIAL PRAYER REQUESTS

This week's memory verse:

_____   _____

_____   _____

Sunday's Reading: **Date:**

God's Message to Me: _____

_____

_____

_____

_____

Monday's Reading: **Date:**

God's Message to Me: _____

_____

_____

_____

_____

Tuesday's Reading: **Date:**

God's Message to Me: _____

_____

_____

_____

_____

Wednesday's Reading: **Date:**

God's Message to Me: _____

_____

_____

_____

_____

Thursday's Reading: **Date:**

God's Message to Me: _____

_____

_____

_____

_____

Friday's Reading: **Date:**

God's Message to Me: _____

_____

_____

_____

_____

Saturday's Reading: **Date:**

God's Message to Me: _____

_____

_____

_____

_____

Blessings and Answers to Prayer

*"…let us offer the sacrifice of praise to God continually…
giving thanks to his name"* (Hebrews 13:15).

Blessings and Answers to Prayer

"…let us offer the sacrifice of praise to God continually…
giving thanks to his name" (Hebrews 13:15).

Blessings and Answers to Prayer

"…let us offer the sacrifice of praise to God continually… giving thanks to his name" (Hebrews 13:15).

Blessings and Answers to Prayer

---

*"...let us offer the sacrifice of praise to God continually...
giving thanks to his name"* (Hebrews 13:15).

Blessings and Answers to Prayer

"...let us offer the sacrifice of praise to God continually... giving thanks to his name" (Hebrews 13:15).

About the Author

Dave Olson became a Baptist preacher in 1993 and has served the Lord in many capacities since that time. After teaching in Bible college, heading up a Christian school, and serving as a pastor, God called Dave into missions. He and his family faithfully served the Lord as missionaries to Zambia, Africa for ten years until a series of ongoing health problems and life-threatening illnesses led to their return in 2012.

In early 2013, the Lord led Dave to focus on a writing ministry, and his books are now used at home and abroad. Dave's experience as an educator and preacher has uniquely equipped him to communicate God's truths to people from every walk of life. In addition to his writing ministry, Dave preaches in revivals, missions conferences, and special meetings across the country.

Visit www.help4Upublications.com for more titles.

Other Titles Available on www.help4Upublications.com

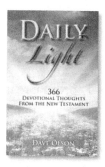

Reading the Word of God is the best way to start your day, and *Daily Light* can make it easier! This book can be used for either personal or family devotions to provide practical insight for daily living. It embarks on a journey through the New Testament, including one thought from an assigned daily Scripture reading designed to share either a challenge or a promise for the day. (204 pages)

Get ready to take a journey through many of the Old Testament books. Morning Light starts in Genesis and includes the books of the Law, History, and Prophets. A practical thought from an assigned daily Scripture reading will challenge you each day. Whether you choose to use Morning Light for personal or family devotions, you will develop a better understanding of the Bible and find practical insight for daily living. (206 pages)

Nobody is exempt from heartaches and hardships. Even great heroes of the faith battled their emotions. Throughout the history of the world, people have battled grief, discouragement, fear, and anxiety. When handled correctly, trials can draw us closer to the Lord and build our faith. Learn how to see your trials as God sees them and react as He has instructed. When you do, you will see brighter days ahead! (188 pages)

Have you ever wondered what God has to say about finances? It's time to learn the proven principles of Scripture concerning money management. Money by the Book provides Biblical solutions for you and your money. Chapters on contentment, giving, saving, getting out of debt, setting up a budget, teaching your children about money, how to reduce spending, and much more! *Money by the Book* is now being used as a textbook in Bible colleges. (246 pages)